GIRL ACTIVIST

Winning strategies from women who've made a difference

By **LOUISA KAMPS**,
SUSANNA DANIEL, and
MICHELLE WILDGEN

Illustrated by
GEORGIA RUCKER

downtown bookworks

Downtown Bookworks Inc.
265 Canal Street, New York, NY 10013
www.downtownbookworks.com

Copyright © 2019 Downtown Bookworks Inc.
Designed and illustrated by Georgia Rucker
Printed in China, April 2019
10 9 8 7 6 5 4 3 2 1

CONTENTS

GIRL ACTIVIST

FOREWORD

You don't have to have special training or degrees to be an activist. You don't even have to be an adult. You just have to care passionately about an issue and get involved.

I became an activist in 2012 after the mass shooting at Sandy Hook Elementary School in Newtown, Connecticut. As a mom of five, I care passionately about the safety of my children. So I created a Facebook page calling on other moms to come together to fight for laws that would make it harder for dangerous people to get guns.

And just like that, I became an activist. Thousands of mothers—and others—wanted to join me in helping to stop gun violence. Together we held rallies and marches, we showed up in statehouses and corporate boardrooms, and we visited our lawmakers in Washington, DC.

I never imagined that my Facebook page would turn into Moms Demand Action for Gun Sense in America, now one of the largest grassroots movements in the nation. Or that we would change so many laws and policies across the country to help stop gun violence.

But it didn't happen overnight. Activism is hard work. It takes a lot of time and effort to create change in a democracy. You have to be patient, knowing that the activism you work on may not be finished in a month, a year, or even during your lifetime. Think of activism as a marathon, not a sprint.

The good news, though, is that you don't have to wait to get started. In fact, you can learn from the stories in this book and apply what you learn to your own activism. When Anne Frank was just 14 years old, she wrote in her diary, "How wonderful it is that nobody need wait a single moment before starting to improve the world."

There are already so many girls your age working to change their neighborhoods, schools, communities—and even the country—for the better. I know you can do that too. What I've learned as an activist is that if you see a problem, you really do have the power to fix it—no matter who you are, how old you are, what your gender is, or where you come from.

So what's next? As you read this book, think about what issues give you goose bumps or make you feel like crying or touch your soul in some way. Then do some research. How is the problem being addressed? How can you help? Can you join existing groups already working on the issue, or do you need to create your own? What skills do you have that will help solve the problem? (By the way, if you can make a call or send an email, you have skills!)

Then jump in. Have conversations with experts. Read up on the issue so you have a basic understanding of its history. Start a Facebook page or a Twitter handle or convene a meeting after school with like-minded peers. Meet the people who have influence over your issue—maybe your school board, your mayor, or your state representatives. And as you learn more about the landscape, you can create a plan of action—just like you do when you have a project due at school.

Just remember that your unique experiences and talents will bring a new and important flair to whatever issue you work on. Be confident in the fact that you offer a new outlook on an issue, even if people have been trying to solve it for centuries. No one in the world will ever do activism exactly like you.

Remember that everything you need to create change already exists inside you. You have compassion, determination, and intelligence—and that's exactly the recipe for becoming a successful activist at any age.

—SHANNON WATTS
Founder, Moms Demand Action for Gun Sense in America

INTRODUCTION

Maybe you've noticed an unfair policy operating at your school or in your neighborhood. Maybe you've learned about an industry practice that is hurting the environment and contributing to climate change. Or maybe you've heard some people saying unkind things about others, based on their gender or the color of their skin.

At times, encountering injustice and intolerance can be so uncomfortable that you may want to put your hands over your ears and close your eyes. But because you care about people and want to make the world a better place, you can't ignore what's happening. To that, we say: Thank you and congratulations. You're already on your way to becoming a great social activist—a girl on a mission to make positive change.

The steps you'll take to create a safer, healthier, kinder, and more equitable society will not only improve many other people's lives but will make your own life richer and more rewarding too. Fighting for a good cause can be challenging. But it's always interesting and, because you're likely to meet cool people through activism, it's often a lot more fun than sitting at home alone in front of the TV.

But what does it really take to build a movement and push for new social, political, environmental, or economic reforms? Organize a protest to bring attention to a worthy cause? Or encourage cranky people with narrow views to think more open-mindedly? Here in *Girl Activist*—a book named to honor the extraordinary courage of the activists we profile, as well as your own budding power to stand up for justice—we offer pages and pages of answers to these questions, and many more.

We dive into what it's like to realize, with striking clarity, that something isn't right. To formulate a clear action plan. To find fellow activist allies you can team up with to trade notes and give each other support. To keep pushing forward—eyes on the prize—even when you face setbacks and make mistakes. (Social activists are human beings, not saints, after all.)

Some of the protesters we profile put their own lives at risk in order to counter violent extremism. The African-American journalist and activist

Ida B. Wells did this by traveling across the Deep South on her own during a time—the 1890s—of intense racism in order to investigate and expose the lynchings, or mob killings, of black people. When Malala Yousafzai, a Pakistani schoolgirl, began to publicly criticize religious militants who were trying to deny girls their basic right to education, she was brutally attacked. Fortunately, Malala survived, and today she's one of the world's most admired human rights activists.

Other activists waded in gradually, starting small initiatives that have become mighty over time. When transgender teen Jazz Jennings started creating low-tech YouTube video diaries about her life, she had no idea that the kind of basic, helpful nuts-and-bolts information she provided would turn out to be tremendously eye-opening for people all over the world who were struggling to understand transgenderism. Alexandra Scott's simple idea to sell lemonade from a stand on her front lawn to raise money for cancer research continues to draw major donations every year.

Some of the girls and women we write about came from families with strong traditions of social activism. Others had no background in political protest but quickly got up to speed after they found out about measures threatening their jobs and communities. Or they were moved to action after learning that the basic rights of women, immigrants, people of color, or people with different abilities were being overlooked and violated. We were struck by how often women and girls have taken bold steps to protect things that are essential for basic healthy living: clean drinking water, fresh food, and oceans and streams that are pure enough for animals and plants to thrive. And we were impressed by how many social media–savvy women are stepping up now to take on leadership roles in important campaigns aimed at stopping gun violence and violence against women. Their fierce determination to fight these scourges in our society is literally awesome to behold.

To show how social activism has evolved, we've written about women who worked in the past and women who are working right now, with all their might, to fight for justice. You may recognize some of the names in this book (Rosa Parks, Eleanor Roosevelt, Emma Watson) and some traditional forms of protest (striking, boycotting, marching, gathering signatures on a petition), but we hope you find some new names

(Amythest Schaber, Betty Kwan Chinn, Jasilyn Charger) and new ideas for successful change-making here (have you ever heard of birddogging?).

We also hope you are inspired to find ways that you can put your own interests and strengths to work. If the arts are your thing, use them: Lady Gaga, Lidiya Yankovskaya, and Sonita Alizadeh have used their musical talents in very different ways to shine a light on suffering communities. Christie Begnell uses her talents as an illustrator to educate people about eating disorders. Maysoon Zayid's tool is comedy. And Madison Stewart? She makes films to change people's minds about sharks. Maybe you're drawn to writing or sharing your thoughts online? Sophie Cruz wrote a letter. Rachel Carson wrote a book. Gloria Steinem started a magazine. Marley Dias's deft use of a hashtag and Yara Shahidi's engaging Instagram posts have shown how you can use social media to call attention to something and make a difference in the world.

There are so many ways to make your mark, from staging a sit-in or giving a speech to registering voters or working with scientists. Judy Heumann gets around in a wheelchair—she has also used it to stop traffic. Lilly Ledbetter used the law to effect change. Tennis was Billie Jean King's path to making a difference. Alicia Garza, Patrisse Khan-Cullors, and Opal Tometi organized a bike ride (among many other things). Aiko Herzig-Yoshinaga relied on her research skills to change the lives of Japanese Americans who suffered terrible discrimination during World War II. LeeAnne Walters used science to successfully argue her points.

And these incredible activists are working around the country and all over the world: LaDonna Redmond grew crops on the West Side of Chicago. Emma González is working for common-sense gun reform in Florida and all over the United States. Wangari Maathai planted trees across Kenya. Melati and Isabel Wijsen are combating plastic waste in Indonesia.

There are so many women here who can inspire you through times of doubt and fear. We hope you'll learn from their stories. Feel free to borrow their tools. Harassment, discrimination, violence, and plain old bad ideas aren't very hard to find these days, unfortunately. But you can start chipping away at any problem you want to fix today. Activism is for everyone. You have all the passion. Now, go out and change the world!

—LOUISA KAMPS

Julia Butterfly Hill

ONE PERSON CAN MAKE A DIFFERENCE

Sometimes a stunt is just a stunt, like when a skydiver dives without a parachute on live television or a tightrope walker crosses between skyscrapers. But sometimes a stunt, if it's timed right and carried out with integrity, can be a meaningful and memorable form of protest—and it can get results.

In 1997, at 23 years old, Julia Butterfly Hill had just recuperated from a bad car accident when she made a decision that would change her life—and the face of environmental activism—forever. It happened in California, where she'd gone to witness the "wisdom, energy, and spirituality" of the redwood forests. There, she met a group of people known as "tree sitters." These folks were living in trees to keep them from being cut down by Pacific Lumber Company.

Butterfly, as she's been called since she was a child, joined the protest. She had never done a "tree sit" before, but when the leaders asked for a volunteer to spend two weeks up 180 feet—about 18 stories—in a giant redwood, she was the only one to raise her hand.

Her first two visits to Luna, as the 1,500-year-old towering redwood was called, lasted only five and six days each. But weeks later, in December 1997, armed with more experience and loads of supplies, Butterfly went back up. This time, she lived up in the tree on two 6-by-6-foot platforms for 738 days. That's more than two years.

Butterfly quickly became an international celebrity. She used a solar-powered cell phone to communicate with reporters and appeared on TV as an "in-tree" correspondent. In the standoff between the lumber company and the forest, Butterfly proved that she would not be the first to back down. Eventually Pacific Lumber caved under the negative publicity. In 1999, the company agreed to preserve a 200-foot buffer zone around Luna. It would keep Luna and other nearby redwoods safe. The company also offered a $50,000 settlement to be donated to California's Humboldt State University for sustainable forestry research.

In December 1999, Butterfly came down from Luna.

Since that time, Butterfly has become a motivational speaker and outspoken activist. Her books *The Legacy of Luna* and *One Makes the Difference* were printed on 100% post-consumer recycled paper with soy-based ink and chlorine-free processing. She donates much of her book earnings to social and environmental causes. Butterfly is car-free, which means she walks, bikes, or uses public transit to get around. She uses a glass jar instead of a plastic water bottle and metal utensils instead of plastic ones. She is also a vegan, which means she doesn't consume animal products of any kind.

GO FOR THE HEADLINES

Life in the tree was harsh. Winter temperatures fell below freezing, with terrible storms and high winds. Lumber company security guards harassed Butterfly from the ground and by helicopter. She battled illness without seeing a doctor or going to a hospital and kept warm by wearing a sleeping bag night and day. She heated meals on a propane stove and exercised by climbing branches. Butterfly sacrificed her comfort to protect her beloved Luna—and to get headlines for her cause.

Other activists have also worked hard to capture the public's interest. Cleve Jones and his fellow gay rights activists created the AIDS Memorial Quilt to draw attention to the devastation of the AIDS epidemic. When they first laid it out in Washington, DC, in 1987, it covered an area larger than a football field. The environmental organization Greenpeace is great at attention-getting stunts. Members have suspended themselves from bridges to block ice-breaking vessels, dragged a mechanical polar bear the size of a double-decker bus through London to call for protecting the Arctic, and staged mock funerals for Earth.

Butterfly is also a US tax resister. Instead of paying taxes to the government, she says she gives the amount she owes to schools and social and environmental programs. The government requires people to pay taxes if they make a certain amount of money, so Butterfly has to keep her income extremely low. "I'm not against paying taxes," she has said. "I believe in what we can do when we pool our money together for the collective good. But the same is true for the collective bad, because our taxes were being spent not only toward war in Iraq but toward war on this planet."

Butterfly's tax resistance is a different kind of stunt and not nearly as high-profile or picturesque as her residency in Luna the redwood. She refers to her do-it-yourself style of activism as a "resolutionary movement." It is based not on anger, she says, but on love. Butterfly believes activism comes from a love of life, from connection with living things. "Every moment of every day, we are looking for ways to be living examples of all that is beautiful and humble and just and incredible about our world," she says.

Living in a tree is the most famous thing Butterfly has done, but it's far from the only thing. "I don't want that on my epitaph," she says, referring to the words written on a person's grave marker. "What I want is: 'This is a person who cared enough about the world to try to make it a better place.'"

"WE ARE THE ANCESTORS OF THE FUTURE. WHAT DO YOU WANT YOUR LEGACY TO BE?"

Wangari Maathai

FIND A SIMPLE SOLUTION WITH **FAR-REACHING, LONG-LASTING EFFECTS**

Growing up in the 1940s, Wangari Maathai was lucky. She lived in a small village in Kenya surrounded by lush forests. The water was clean. The soil was rich, supporting a wide variety of crops along with nutritious wild fruits and vegetables. "It was heaven. We wanted for nothing," she once said.

At a time when many girls weren't educated, Wangari's family also took the unusual step of sending her to school. She was a terrific student. In 1960, she was one of 300 Kenyan high school graduates who (along with Barack Obama's father) won a scholarship to study in the United States. She earned a master's degree in biology from the University of Pittsburgh, then went on to become the first woman in East Africa to earn a PhD. After she graduated from the University of Nairobi in 1971 with her doctorate, she ran its department of veterinary anatomy and became an associate professor at the university—two more firsts for any African woman in the region.

But knowing how fortunate she'd been also made Wangari eager to help other people. While researching a disease that affects cattle, she traveled to many Kenyan communities, some that she had not seen since she was a girl. She found that they had gone from being full of healthy green plants and trees to almost desertlike as a result of deforestation. (When forests disappear, so do the streams and springs that flow out of them.) Women were traditionally in charge of planting food and gathering wood for fuel, so Wangari knew that living in dry, barren land was especially stressful for them. As she explained, when women "lack wood fuel, water, food, and fodder," they find themselves "in a vicious cycle of debilitating poverty, lost self-confidence, and a never-ending struggle to meet their most basic needs."

Luckily, Wangari, a scientist with enormous spirit and determination, came up with a creative, low-cost way to reverse that cycle. In 1977, working with the National Council of Women of Kenya, she launched the Green Belt Movement (GBM), a program that pays women a small stipend for planting tree seedlings. Wangari and her coworkers asked companies, nonprofits, and other organizations to sponsor the trees. Grants and donations help to keep the movement going.

It is a genius fix that accomplishes several goals at once: the trees help to stop soil erosion, provide shade, and create a renewable source for firewood. They also reduce the amount of carbon dioxide in the air, which protects the climate. To date, GBM partners have planted more than 52 million seedlings! And just as importantly,

WOMEN WARRIORS FOR PEACE

Swedish businessman Alfred Nobel passed away in 1896, leaving behind a vast fortune that he wanted to be used to fund prizes in different fields. The Nobel Peace Prize is given to the people and organizations that have done the most to support friendship between nations, fight for human rights, or advance the causes of disarmament and world peace. Wangari was the 12th woman to win the prestigious award (17 women and 89 men have won to date), which includes a cash prize of nearly $1 million. Some of the other incredible female recipients of the prize are pioneer social reformer Jane Addams and Mother Teresa, the missionary nun who dedicated her life to helping the poor in the slums of Calcutta, India. Rigoberta Menchú earned the prize for her work for social justice in Guatemala, and Tawakkol Karman, from Yemen, was recognized for her fight for freedom of expression and women's rights in the Arab world.

giving women a source of ongoing income and the ability to provide for their families by growing crops gives them renewed dignity. "Tree planting empowered these women because it was not a complicated thing. It was something that they could do and see the results of. They could, by their own actions, improve the quality of their lives," she said.

Wangari, who died of cancer in 2011, frequently chastised commercial tea, coffee, and sugarcane plantations that took over land that local farmers had used to grow their own food, creating hardships for many families. She also enraged politicians with her sharp criticism of government policies that encouraged deforestation and real estate development of public park land. At times, she was even beaten and jailed for her outspokenness.

But many Kenyan women and their families continue to benefit from her bighearted tree-planting plan and its many positive outcomes. In 2004, Wangari became the first African woman to win a Nobel Peace Prize. And, as the committee honoring her said about her then, "She has taken a holistic approach to sustainable development that embraces democracy, human rights, and women's rights in particular. She thinks globally and acts locally."

"WHEN WE CAN GIVE OURSELVES FOOD, FIREWOOD, AND HELP TO NURTURE SOIL FOR PLANTING AND CLEAN WATER, THEN WE **BEGIN TO ROLL POVERTY BACK.**"

Dolores Huerta

TEACH TO BRING CHANGE

When racial and ethnic prejudice flourishes in the United States, it's because we're not recording and teaching history as well as we should, says Dolores Huerta. She's an 88-year-old civil rights icon who has fought fearlessly to improve the terrible working conditions of migrant farm workers. "We never teach that Native Americans were the first slaves, that African slaves built the White House and the Congress—that all this land was tilled, the railroads were built, the construction was done by Mexican immigrants, Chinese, Japanese, Filipinos," Dolores observed in 2017, just as President Trump was threatening (not for the last time) to shut down Congress if it wouldn't fund his notorious border wall.

In the early 1950s, Dolores was working as a schoolteacher in the agricultural community of Stockton, California. She became alarmed by the dire poverty her students—many of them the children of migrant workers—were living in. She joined forces with another local activist, Cesar Chavez, to form the National Farm Workers Association (now known as the United Farm Workers of America union). Dolores and Cesar lobbied politicians, negotiated with growers, and organized migrant farm laborers to fight for fair wages and safe working conditions. They achieved many things, including requirements for growers to give their farm workers regular breaks and pay them minimum wage.

Often, however, Dolores had to become a teacher all over again to help the growers understand how they could still do better. Once she was negotiating with a grower who felt he'd already taken a big step by giving his workers water. She then calmly explained that the water was warm, the workers had no individual cups, *and* the last tub he supplied had a dead mouse in it. Dolores said that being a woman might have helped her. "I think the fact that I was presenting some of these issues to them, it helped the growers to accept them. If I had been male, I would have made them feel these were weapons, not just facts."

Dolores also helped teach Americans critical lessons about the food they eat. She got consumers to think about the people who plant and harvest their crops. In the 1960s and 1970s, she and Cesar spearheaded a series of national boycotts against grapes and lettuce. The boycotts brought much-needed attention to farm workers' ongoing demands for safer working conditions and better wages—and some of these demands were ultimately met because of their actions. The boycotts also helped people all across the country appreciate the major impact their votes can have in changing how migrant workers are treated. And she's not just talking about the votes made in actual polling places. She's also referring to the choices consumers make in grocery stores.

WORKING TOGETHER

Much of Dolores's success as a labor leader has happened as a result of bringing people together in collective action. In a 2012 speech, she spoke about the right to freedom of association, which is an essential part of the freedom of speech guaranteed by the US Constitution. "The freedom of association means that people can come together in organization to fight for solutions to the problems they confront in their communities," she said. "The great social justice changes in our country have happened when people came together, organized, and took direct action. It is this right that sustains and nurtures our democracy today." Dolores argued that the civil rights movement, the labor movement, the women's movement, and the movement for equality for "our LGBT brothers and sisters" are all examples of what people can do when they work together.

Today, as founder and president of the Dolores Huerta Foundation, Dolores is devoted to helping educate young people from immigrant backgrounds about politics and social inequality, the vulnerabilities they face, how to protect themselves, and how to build better lives by getting involved in political action. It's a fitting new chapter for the onetime schoolteacher who really knows how to make the most important lessons sink in.

During the early farm strikes, Dolores came up with a slogan *Sí se puede*—Spanish for "Yes we can." The slogan helped to make farm workers and boycotters feel more bold than they might have without those inspiring words ringing in their ears. The slogan helped to unify them. Years later, Barack Obama borrowed Dolores's slogan during his presidential campaigns. And when he awarded her the Presidential Medal of Freedom in 2012, he made sure to credit *her* as the creator of the famous workers' rallying cry, rather than Cesar, who's often been given credit for coming up with it. "Dolores was very gracious when I told her I had stolen her slogan," Obama joked. But she was glad to have him revise the historical record and—finally—give her the credit she was due. "I always thought it was wrong for me to take credit for the work that I did," Dolores said in a 2017 documentary about her work and life. "I don't think that anymore."

> **"I HOPE MY LEGACY WILL BE THAT I WAS AN ORGANIZER— THAT I HAVE PASSED ON THE MIRACLES THAT CAN BE ACCOMPLISHED WHEN PEOPLE COME TOGETHER, THE THINGS THEY CAN CHANGE."**

Emma Watson

DELIVER A SPEECH AND
MAKE IT COUNT

Like many other women and girls, British actor and United Nations (UN) Women Goodwill Ambassador Emma Watson knows what it's like to be treated a certain way based on her sex. The first time she felt confused about how girls are "supposed" to act, she was eight years old. In a speech she delivered at the UN in 2014, she explained that while putting on a play with friends, she noticed that she got called "bossy" when she offered directing tips. She also noticed that the boys in the group never got slapped with that label.

Emma's UN speech, an electrifying personal testimony, instantly went viral. In it, she also noted that she was only 14 years old (three years into her remarkable career playing Hermione Granger in the Harry Potter movie series) when she realized that bloggers, magazine editors, and talk show hosts were often more interested in discussing her looks than they were in highlighting her work and ideas.

Emma was speaking at an event marking the launch of HeForShe, a UN program that aims to get men involved in the fight for gender equality. She was 24 at the time and had recently appeared in a string of hit movies, including *The Perks of Being a Wallflower* and *The Bling Ring*. Emma had the good fortune to study at universities where, as she says, women learn "that their brain power is valued." She'd just graduated from college a few months before. She'd also traveled to Bangladesh and Zambia to help promote education for girls and worked on other human rights initiatives. But despite all of her impressive accomplishments (and privileges), Emma was nervous. It was as if she was confessing a dangerous secret when she told the audience: "I decided I was a feminist, and this seemed uncomplicated to me. But my recent research has shown me that *feminism* has become an unpopular word."

However, the passion and occasional catch in her voice only underscored the truth of her message: It's time for the world to stop thinking of feminists as "man-hating" zealots and start making gender equality a priority, for the good of everyone in society. "Both men and women should feel free to be sensitive. Both men and women should feel free to be strong. . . . It is time we all perceive gender on a spectrum, not as two opposing sets of ideals," she said. She ended her speech with an emotional appeal for men to call out sexist attitudes toward women when they see them in their own schools, workplaces, or social circles: "I'm inviting you to step forward, to be seen, and to ask yourself, 'If not me, who? If not now, when?'"

OUR SHARED SHELF

Working with UN Women inspired Emma to read books and essays on equality, feminism, human rights, and sisterhood. To encourage lively discussion, she started a feminist book club on Goodreads.com called Our Shared Shelf. Membership is free and open to anyone who is interested. Some of the books the club has read together include *The Hate U Give* by Angie Thomas, *The Radium Girls* by Kate Moore, and *Why I'm No Longer Talking to White People About Race* by Reni Eddo-Lodge.

People from around the world—including Prince Harry, Hillary Clinton, and Desmond Tutu, the South African human rights and anti-apartheid activist—quickly signed on to voice their support for HeForShe. Malala Yousafzai said later that seeing Emma stand up and identify herself as a feminist gave her the courage to call herself a feminist too. And to Emma's delight, as she later noted, even "some 15-year-old boys" started "writing in to national newspapers deploring female discrimination" after they'd seen her speech.

Of course, not everyone was pleased. Emma also received threats in the wake of her now famous HeForShe launch speech. But if holdouts for old-school sexism "were trying to put me off, it did the opposite," she's said.

These days, Emma continues to push for change through HeForShe, encouraging husbands, young men, CEOs, and business leaders to make concrete commitments to gender equality. She also lends her star power to different campaigns dedicated to stopping violence and harassment against women.

In 2018, Emma posted a picture of herself on Instagram that makes it clear that she is now 100% comfortable defining herself as a feminist. "Girls just wanna have fundamental human rights" was stitched across the back of the red satin jacket she wore in the photo. At a certain point, the actor-turned-activist described how she became a fully committed champion of women's rights.

> "**YOU'RE NOT ALONE.** AND EVEN IF YOU ARE, IN A PARTICULAR MOMENT . . . REMEMBER YOU COME FROM A LONG LINE OF FEMINISTS WHO DID THIS WORK, IN THE OUTSIDE WORLD BUT ALSO INSIDE THEMSELVES."

She said, "I was like, 'Go for it! Say what you need to say. Other people's perception of you can't be the most important thing. You have to let your perception of yourself have a lot more weight.'"

Clara Lemlich

SHOW THAT THERE IS **STRENGTH** IN NUMBERS

Today we have labor laws to protect workers. But at the beginning of the 20th century, thousands of men and women—most of them immigrants—worked long hours in unsafe conditions in American factories. Clara Lemlich, whose family came to New York City in 1903 when she was just 16 years old, was one of those workers. At the Gotham shirtwaist factory, she labored 11 hours a day, six days a week, for very little pay. "They treat workers like machines," said Clara about the factory.

Clara joined the International Ladies' Garment Workers' Union and frequently protested on picket lines. Within a few years, she'd been arrested 17 times and even beaten by the police, who broke six of her ribs. In November of 1909, at age 23, she found herself speaking in front of thousands of unhappy laborers at a rally in downtown Manhattan. "I am one of those who suffers from the abuses described here," she said to the crowd, "and I move that we go on a general strike." This was a shocking statement, especially from a woman. A strike meant that thousands of people would refuse to work, and factories would have to pause operations or give the workers what they wanted.

What followed Clara's declaration became known as the Uprising of the 20,000. At the time, it was the largest strike by women workers ever in the United States. The goal was to make workplaces safer, workdays shorter, and wages higher. The strike lasted three months and was a big step in the right direction, though there was still a long way to go. (A year later, a deadly fire at the Triangle Shirtwaist Factory exposed the persistence of unsafe working conditions for women in factories.) But the wave of activism had another consequence. As a newspaper noted in 1910, "These young, inexperienced girls have proved that women can strike, and strike successfully."

Later, Clara would say that she felt she had no choice but to speak out when so many others were holding their tongues. "I had fire in my mouth," she said.

After the Uprising, Clara was blacklisted from factory work, which meant no one would hire her. So she started organizing Brooklyn housewives and mothers to protest for affordable food and housing.

Clara and her husband Joe raised their three children in an activist home, demonstrating every day how collective action can inspire change. At the time of her death in 1982 at age 96, Clara was still an activist. She led a produce boycott at her retirement home and helped the staff to organize. For Clara, activism wasn't a job or a hobby—it was a way of life.

> **"I THINK THE WOMEN WHO BUY AND WEAR THE BEAUTIFUL CLOTHES DO NOT KNOW HOW IT IS FOR THE GIRL WHO MAKES THEM—WHAT CONDITIONS SHE HAS—OR THEY WOULD CARE AND WOULD TRY TO HELP HER."**

READY TO VOTE TOO

One of Clara's most personal causes was women's suffrage, or right to vote. "The manufacturer has a vote; the bosses have votes; the foremen have votes; the inspectors have votes. The working girl has no vote," she wrote in *Good Housekeeping* in 1912. But at the time, some people in the labor movement considered her suffrage activism to be a step too far. She was ousted from a labor group she'd helped create for her stance on suffrage.

Alex Scott

RAISE MONEY FOR YOUR **CAUSE**

Alexandra "Alex" Scott had cancer most of her life. She was diagnosed with neuroblastoma, a form of childhood cancer impacting nerve cells, just before her first birthday. The disease made it hard for her to walk, and treatments often left her weak. But this never dented her determination to help other children with cancer—in the sweetest, simplest, and most inspiring way imaginable.

In 2000, when Alex was four years old, she received an experimental treatment that made her feel better. She wanted more children to benefit from new treatments. So she decided to raise money for cancer research. How would she do it? By selling lemonade, naturally! She set up her first stand in front of her house, pouring drinks from a pitcher set out on her plastic toy picnic table. And Alex, a major fan of Junie B. Jones books and her cat Herbert, surprised no one more than her parents, Liz and Jay. They assumed she'd take in only a handful of bills and change, but she raised $2,000 that day. "It was amazing. People came, some with smiles, some with tears, but they kept coming and coming! I had never seen anything like it before," Jay recalled. As her mom was tucking her into bed that night, Alex told her that the success of her lemonade sale was the best thing that ever happened to her.

ALEX'S
Lemonade Stand
to benefit pediatric
cancer research

"When life gives you lemons, make lemonade" became Alex's mantra, and she went on to sell many more gallons of the stuff. As word of her sales spread, more people flocked to her stands. One generous customer even paid her $500 for a cup, making that the most expensive single cup she ever sold. Children around the country started setting up their own lemonade stands and sending Alex contributions with their profits.

In 2004, when Alex was eight, her treatments unfortunately stopped working, and her health declined. But according to Jay, this made her "even more determined to change things for other kids with cancer." During an appearance on *The Oprah Winfrey Show* that June, Alex was frail but smiling. She explained her goal to raise $1 million for cancer research that year. When her father asked her how she would raise so much money, she said, "If everyone has lemonade stands, I think we can do it."

Thanks to her own sales and thousands of other kids' hard work hawking lemonade, plus donations from corporate sponsors, she exceeded her goal in July. Alex died two weeks later, on August 1, 2004.

"I RAISE MONEY BECAUSE IT'S HELPING PEOPLE."

But her sweet and simple commitment to helping others continues to inspire enormous generosity. Many kids have realized that if Alex could raise money for cancer research by selling lemonade, then they can too. After Alex passed away, her parents founded a charity, Alex's Lemonade Stand Foundation. To date, it has raised more than $150 million to fund innovative studies and help children and families dealing with cancer, making it one of the most successful nonprofits supporting medical research today.

Ida B. Wells

DARE TO **TELL THE TRUTH**

In 1892, a 29-year-old journalist named Ida B. Wells received terrible news. Three friends of hers in Memphis, Tennessee, had been lynched. Her friends were black men who owned a grocery store in town. They were murdered by a mob of white men who couldn't stand to see them prospering in the community.

Yet rather than go mute in her grief and anger, Ida wrote a series of fiery articles on the crime in the *Free Speech and Headlight*, a local newspaper that she partly owned. She demanded that the killers be arrested. She urged black people to leave town or stop riding the white-owned streetcar to protest the killings. It was one of the first economic boycotts ever organized in the South, and it worked. The streetcar company experienced serious financial strain once black customers stopped buying rides.

But Ida quickly faced consequences for her outspokenness. White newspaper writers called her a "black scoundrel." Rumors floated around Memphis that a group of men were eager to hang her. And, a few weeks after her friends were killed, while she was in Philadelphia for a church convention, a gang of men broke into the offices of the *Free Speech* and trashed them. These men were determined to silence her, one way or the other.

Fearing for her safety, Ida stayed in New York for a while, then resettled in Chicago. But the events she witnessed and chronicled that year "opened my eyes to what lynching really was," she later wrote in her autobiography, *Crusade for Justice*. One of the claims people used to justify lynchings was that they could stop black men from committing crimes against white women. But that was just "an excuse ," Ida wrote, "to get rid of Negroes who were acquiring wealth and property and thus keep the race terrorized."

Ida was born into slavery in 1862, during the Civil War, just six months before President Abraham Lincoln signed the Emancipation Proclamation. (This proclamation freed the slaves in the Southern states that seceded from the Union, including Ida's home state of Tennessee.) By the time Ida was an adult, many black people felt disillusioned and angry about civil rights protections they'd already gained and lost. The Civil Rights Act of 1875, for example, vowed to protect all citizens'—including African Americans'—access to hotels, trains, theaters, and other public spaces. But in 1883, the Supreme Court nullified many of the act's protections, paving the way for antiblack discrimination and racial injustice to return with force. During a time of deep antiblack sentiment, Ida risked her life not only by writing about the lynching of her friends in Memphis but also by traveling afterward to many small towns across the South, where

REVEALING UNCOMFORTABLE TRUTHS

Investigative journalists like Ida do in-depth research to report on controversial subjects or cover stories that usually reveal things that have been concealed. Five years before Ida got the horrific news that her friends had been murdered, investigative reporter Nellie Bly went undercover in a mental institution to expose the brutal conditions faced by the patients. Shortly after that, Ida Tarbell became well known for her exposé of the Standard Oil Company published between 1902 and 1904. More recently, Veronica Guerin dug deep into the stories of Irish drug gangs, and Rosario Mosso Castro covered the Mexican cartels. Other investigative journalists include Barbara Ehrenreich, who published a book about the lives of the working poor after a three-month stint working minimum-wage jobs, and Jane Mayer, who has taken on topics from how right-wing billionaires use their money to influence academics and politics to the US government's use of drones and torture in the War on Terror.

she investigated the brutal murders of other black men, women, and children.

But Ida, who worked as a teacher before taking up writing, didn't stop there. She traveled to speaking engagements across the United States and Europe, making sure that people everywhere were educated about the horrors of lynching. She called out the crime to make it part of the national conversation. She also fought against school segregation in Chicago, organized campaigns against mass incarceration, and pushed for women's suffrage.

In 1895, Ida married Ferdinand L. Barnett, a Chicago lawyer and activist. Some of her fellow activist friends—including Susan B. Anthony—worried that marriage might slow her down and blunt the righteous anger that made her such a fierce and effective fighter for social justice. (Ida "didn't suffer fools, and she saw fools everywhere," her grandson once noted.) But Ferdinand did something that was unusual for a man at that time—he took on more household chores so that his wife could continue her important work.

And fortunately, Ida's commitment to fighting for social justice never waned. Her powerful essays and booming speeches made her the most famous black woman in the United States in her lifetime, historians say. Methods that she pioneered for protesting racism were used over and over during the civil rights movement of the 1950s and 1960s. She understood that "the price of liberty is eternal vigilance," and her example continues to inspire young journalists and activists around the world.

"TELL THE WORLD THE FACTS."

Sonita Alizadeh

FIND THE **RIGHT TOOL** FOR YOUR MESSAGE

Every two seconds, in countries around the world, a girl younger than 18 is married. When this happens, the girl almost always loses the opportunity to become educated and is often put at great risk of illness and abuse. Many of these marriages are forced.

Sonita Alizadeh was born in Afghanistan but spent much of her childhood in Iran, where her family fled to escape the Taliban, a strict religious group. Her family first considered marrying her off at the age of 10. Lucky for Sonita, the proposed arrangement fell through.

In Iran, Sonita had no official documentation, so she couldn't go to school. Instead, she worked cleaning bathrooms. In her spare time, she watched music videos. Her favorites were by Eminem, Drake, Rihanna, and an Iranian rapper called Yas. She loved the beat and urgency of the music, even when she couldn't understand the words. Soon, Sonita started writing poems and rap lyrics in her own language. To Sonita, rap was more powerful than pop music. She didn't think pop could contain a story as challenging and emotional as her own. Around this time, Sonita was introduced to an Iranian filmmaker named Rokhsareh Ghaem Maghami, who was impressed by Sonita's music and ambition. She started following Sonita with a video camera and, one day, while Rokhsareh was filming, Sonita's family started talking about selling her into marriage. Sonita's brother

was going to marry soon. And they needed the money to pay a dowry—or wedding gift—to Sonita's brother's bride. In the film, Sonita listens, sad and worried, as her mother talks about selling her. She knew even in that moment that she needed to protest the marriage and rebel against her parents. But she wasn't angry at her parents. Her mother had been married at age 13—she didn't know any other way.

Naturally, Sonita's protest took the form of a rap music video. "Brides for Sale," which she made with Rokhsareh's help, opens with Sonita in a black hijab (a type of headscarf Muslim women wear) with a barcode on her forehead, as if she's a product in a store. She starts the song in a quiet voice, saying, "Let me whisper to you my words, so no one hears that I'm speaking about the selling of girls." A few lines later, she's rapping in a strong, loud voice. "I'm 15 years old, from Herat," raps Sonita. "A few have come as suitors and I am confused. . . . They sell girls for money. No right to choose."

Women aren't allowed to sing by themselves in public in Iran, so Sonita and Rokhsareh made the video in secret. But once it was out in the world, the video took on a life of its own. Soon it was watched by half a million viewers across the world.

A few weeks later, Sonita was contacted by a social activist organization called the Strongheart Group, which offered to pay for her student visa to come to the United States and attend a private

"FIND A MESSAGE THAT YOU MUST SHARE, AND THEN DO IT IN A WAY THAT IS **AUTHENTIC TO YOU**. MY WAY IS USING RAP, BUT THERE ARE A MILLION DIFFERENT WAYS TO SHARE YOUR MESSAGE."

high school on scholarship. Sonia accepted the offer right away, without even telling her parents. They didn't understand her decision until they watched her video and heard her music. "In Afghanistan, they hear my songs from TV, from radios," Sonita said. "Now they realize, as a girl I have power."

Sonita quickly learned English and got great grades in high school. In her graduation speech, she said to her classmates, "I want you to believe in yourself and know that you can make a difference in this world. Maybe not today, maybe not tomorrow. But soon. . . . I care about child marriage, my tool is rap. What do you care about? And what is your tool?"

Today, at age 21, Sonita spends her time performing, speaking out against child marriage, and working in the studio on new songs. She has performed at the State Department's International Women of Courage Awards ceremony and been interviewed by Chelsea Clinton. Rokhsareh's documentary about her life, *Sonita*, won awards at the 2016 Sundance Film Festival. Sonita has also helped develop a lesson plan for teaching high school students around the world about child marriage and how to fight it.

Sonita's message for other girls who want to create change is to first and foremost believe in yourself. Be strong, she says. "Change can be overwhelming and scary, especially if you are trying to change your own life or an old tradition like child marriage. Begin simply. Imagine something different. Then believe it is possible. Next, take small steps toward that goal."

CHALLENGING TRADITION

Sonita knows that it will be difficult to stop child marriage because it is rooted in tradition and poverty. To succeed, she believes people must work on many levels. Families and even the girls themselves need to know there are other options. Communities and religious leaders need to be encouraged to give up the destructive tradition. Governments and organizations need to support programs that help end child marriage, especially programs created and run by local people. And then lawmakers must create and pass laws worldwide to make child marriage illegal. One day, Sonita may be one of those lawmakers! She hopes to attend law school.

Melati and Isabel Wijsen

FIND **INSPIRATION** IN MOVEMENTS THAT CAME BEFORE

Sisters Melati and Isabel Wijsen were kids when they saw a problem around them, on the Indonesian island of Bali. Thanks to tourism and the constant use of plastics, their tranquil island home was generating a shocking amount of plastic bags, bottles, wrappers, and more. In fact, it was creating as much as 24,000 cubic feet (680 cubic meters) of waste each day. That amount of plastic waste can take up as much space as a 14-story building.

The plastic was causing serious problems. People littered. Plastic was filling the ocean and washing up on the beaches. Tortoises were getting wrapped in plastic nets. Birds and fish were eating plastics, which meant that the humans who ate local birds and fish were eating plastic too. On top of that, a lot of people didn't realize that their habit of burning plastics to get rid of them was releasing cancer-causing chemicals in the smoke. "We used to have things like food wrapped in banana leaves, and people can just throw it away because it is organic and completely decomposable," Melati has said. "But now the packaging has changed to plastic, [and] people still have the mind-set that they can simply throw it away. It is definitely not good."

The plastic problem was clear, but the solution wasn't so obvious. At school, Melati and Isabel had studied enough activists to know they didn't want to wait until adulthood to transform the world around them. When the girls learned that the small East African country of Rwanda had already banned bags made of polyethylene, a common type of plastic film, in 2008, they were inspired. They decided that "Bali should get on its game," said Melati.

And so, in 2013, when Melati was 12 and Isabel 10, they launched Bye Bye Plastic Bags (BBPB). For the first year and a half, their cause didn't get much notice. Even with a petition signed by more than 100,000 people, they still had not caught the attention of the government. The governor of Bali, I Made Mangku Pastika, had said the garbage that washed up on the beaches with each year's monsoons was just a natural phenomenon. Melati and Isabel were delivering letters to the governor's office every day without results. It was clear that BBPB needed a new plan.

They found it on a family trip to India in 2014. The girls visited the home of Mahatma Gandhi, who protested British rule in India with peaceful protest marches and hunger strikes. And the visit gave them another idea. Isabel remembered, "We said, 'Mum, Dad, we are going on a food strike.'"

THINK BIG!

Melati and Isabel hoped to grab the government's attention by gathering a million signatures on a petition. But it was slow going. Someone mentioned the huge number of people who went through the Bali airport every day. So the sisters went to the airport and persuaded a manager to allow them to collect signatures at the departure gate. They got 1,000 signatures in their first hour! (BBPB can no longer do this because of airport security, but it was a big idea that paid off at the time.)

But it wasn't quite that simple. "School, teachers, people around the world all thought we were insane," said Melati. They agreed that they would not eat from dawn to dusk, a practice called *mogok makan*, until they could meet with the governor to make a case for ending Bali's use of plastic bags. Their food fast immediately got attention on social media. The police visited the Wijsen family's home and were surprised to discover the campaign really was being run by two young girls. Within 48 hours, the governor agreed to meet with them.

They had finally found support for their environmental goals! The governor signed a memorandum of understanding to help Bali end its use of plastic bags by 2018. Melati and Isabel then worked with the government to develop programs that help reduce plastic bag use. BBPB has created an educational booklet for elementary students about pollution and waste management. BBPB also distributes instructions for making reusable bags.

> **"YOU CAN'T DO IT BY YOURSELF. PULL TOGETHER A TEAM OF LIKE-MINDED PEOPLE TO HELP BRING YOUR IDEA INTO REALITY."**
> —MELATI WIJSEN

Melati and Isabel have expanded BBPB's team far beyond Bali. There are now 25 teams around the world. Isabel and Melati have given a TED Talk (a short speech describing new, surprising, and exciting ideas) in London and spoken to world leaders at the United Nations in New York. Next the girls hope to persuade Indonesian president Joko Widodo to ban single-use plastics altogether. The sisters are hopeful. A recent study showed that 97% of the people surveyed were okay with a policy that would make people pay for their plastic bags. "It indicates that people in Indonesia are aware of the plastic problem," said Isabel, and that they want to fix it.

And although Bali did not achieve its goal to end plastic bag use by 2018, there is good news. In December 2018, Bali got a new governor—one who pledged to help preserve the environment. Governor Wayan Koster announced that the government would ban most single-use plastics by mid-2019. Melati says she has learned it takes time to create change. "Dancing with politicians—it's three steps forward, two steps back, and then again and again," she said. "But I understand that we need to be doing it together."

Choose REUSABLE TOTES

Judy Heumann

GET IN THE WAY OF DISCRIMINATION

Sometimes you have to get in the way to make a difference. Judy Heumann takes this idea literally. For many years, the government tried to ignore the rights of people like Judy, who has used a wheelchair since a childhood bout with polio. But it's hard to ignore groups of people when they take over your space—and that's just what Judy and other disability advocates did.

In 1972, Congress passed the Rehabilitation Act, a bill that would have helped many people with disabilities or chronic illnesses. Section 504 of the bill was particularly important to Judy. It prohibited discrimination against people because of their disabilities. But instead of signing it into law, President Richard Nixon vetoed the bill. In response, Judy and other activists staged a sit-in at the Federal Office Building in Manhattan. Their action wasn't enough to make the government acknowledge the rights of disabled people. So the group tried other tactics. They took to the streets, some in wheelchairs and some on crutches. Judy and the others blocked traffic downtown. Then they headed up to 45th street and used their bodies to shut down Madison Avenue for nearly an hour during rush hour.

Eventually, under pressure, Nixon signed the legislation he'd originally vetoed. It was a huge victory for disability rights activists—but for years it didn't have any effect. The government didn't release any specific regulations to make Section 504 a reality. So in April 1977, Judy and more than 150 people decided to force the issue. Inspired by successful demonstrations against racial discrimination, Judy and her fellow activists took over the San Francisco office of the US Department of Health, Education and Welfare (HEW). Judy described the crowd: "Blind people, deaf people, wheelchair users, disabled veterans, people with developmental and psychiatric disabilities and many others all came together" to demand that the secretary of HEW sign the regulations to actually enforce the law.

All over the country, people with disabilities occupied buildings in protest. Most demonstrations lasted a few days. But in San Francisco, activists stayed for days . . . then weeks. No one took them seriously for a while. "At the start of our demonstration at the HEW offices, officials treated us with condescension, giving us cookies and punch as if we were on some kind of field trip," Judy later said.

The government got the picture soon enough. For 25 days, the protesters stayed in the building. They didn't go home to change clothes. They didn't go out for groceries. They didn't go home to sleep at night. The building's sinks became showers. Other local activists like the Black Panthers brought in food and supplies. "We will no longer allow the government to oppress disabled individuals," Judy told the media and government leaders two weeks into the occupation. "We want the law enforced. We want no more segregation." Shortly after that, Judy and a small group of her fellow protesters flew to Washington, DC, to ratchet up the pressure.

After nearly four weeks, the activists won their battle. The HEW secretary signed the regulations. Judy said, "We demonstrated to the entire nation that disabled people could take control over our own lives and take leadership in the struggle for equality." The victory also helped lead to the Americans with Disabilities Act in 1990, which demanded even stronger protections.

Judy admits she still feels "impatience and a feeling of great urgency." She says, "One in four people in the United States have a disability, yet many people are still embarrassed or fearful of identifying with pride that they have a disability." She wants people with disabilities, even ones with "an invisible disability, such as anxiety or depression, or sickle cell anemia, or diabetes" to "speak up, fight bullying, be proud, and come together to openly discuss your vision for a future where all people are treated equally and are respected for who they are."

The struggle for equality isn't over. But the effects of Judy's activism are easy to find: in accessible buses and trains, closed captioning on TV, ramps in schools and on sidewalks and streets, and advances in technology that help people with disabilities.

> **"BEING RESILIENT IS NOT ALWAYS EASY, AND WE DON'T WIN ALL OUR BATTLES, BUT TOMORROW IS ANOTHER DAY TO KEEP UP THE FIGHT."**

A LIFELONG ADVOCATE

Along with her parents, Judy has been fighting for her rights since she was a child. After being told that Judy couldn't attend public school because her wheelchair would get in the way (they said she was a fire hazard), her parents stood up to the school system. Finally, when she was nine years old, Judy was permitted to go to school. "From my parents I learned to never take 'no' for an answer," said Judy. "They set an example for me that I proudly started taking on more and more when I was in my late teens."

When Judy was denied a job as a teacher because of her disability, she sued. She won the lawsuit and became the first wheelchair-using teacher in the New York City public schools. After that, she founded a civil rights organization called Disabled in Action, joined the Center for Independent Living, and even worked for the federal government. Judy still takes part in protests.

LeeAnne Walters

GET **SCIENCE** ON YOUR SIDE

In sports, referees blow a whistle when there's foul play. In life, people who call attention to illegal or unethical activities in organizations are known as *whistleblowers*.

Back in 2014, LeeAnne Walters had no idea she would become a whistleblower. At the time, she was a stay-at-home mother of four in Flint, Michigan, and she noticed that her three-year-old twins were getting rashes on their skin and her daughter's hair was coming out in clumps. Her teenage son was having blurry vision and kidney problems. LeeAnne's own eyelashes were falling out, and her hair was thinning. What was going on?

Then the tap water in the Walters home started to flow brown. First it happened only once or twice, briefly, but then it started happening more and more. LeeAnne, who believes in trusting one's instincts, put two and two together: the problem was in the water.

LeeAnne repeatedly took her questions to city and state officials, but they ignored her, made excuses, lied to her, threatened her, and eventually even offered to give her family money. They said they would fix her pipes if she would sign a waiver that cleared the city of any blame. LeeAnne tried again and again to find answers, and again and again she was shut down. "The state and the city discredited us every which way they could," said LeeAnne in an interview. "The media wouldn't listen to us. We didn't take the money [they offered] . . . because we knew what our family was going through, and we were trying to stop it from happening to anyone else."

LeeAnne was frustrated. "How do we make them listen?" she asked herself. "How do we make them take us seriously? How do we make them care?" There was so much evidence that something was wrong with the water supply, but everyone in the government—and even her own family's pediatrician—told her that she was overreacting or imagining things.

"BEING AN ACTIVIST IS A JUGGLING ACT BETWEEN EMOTION AND LOGIC. YOU HAVE TO LEARN WHEN AND WHERE EACH OF THESE APPLY IN DIFFERENT AREAS OF THE FIGHT."

"We all started brainstorming on it," LeeAnne said, "and we decided that we needed to get to the science of it, because you can't argue with science." LeeAnne had a high school degree and training as a medical assistant, but she didn't know much about water. So she got to work. She stayed up nights and spent weekends learning everything she could about how the city's water was processed and filtered, and what might be going wrong. She attended public meetings and talked to other residents, and it turned out that her family was not alone.

Finally, she persuaded the city to test the water in her home. The tests revealed that the level of lead, which is toxic when touched or digested, was way too high. All of her family's health problems suddenly made sense: they had been poisoned.

State officials were still insisting LeeAnne's water was safe, however, so she cast a wider net. She contacted a regional manager of the Environmental Protection Agency (EPA) named Miguel Del Toral and a Virginia Tech professor and civil engineer named Marc Edwards. Unlike everyone else she'd asked for help, these two believed her, and they joined in her fight. Together, they figured out that the city wasn't applying corrosion controls to prevent lead from leaching out of pipes and into the water supply. The city was also using tests with loopholes that kept real lead amounts from being recorded.

LeeAnne and her team hit the pavement. They spent more than 100 hours per week collecting more than 800 water samples from homes around Flint. The test results revealed the problem was even worse than she'd imagined: one in six homes had lead levels that exceeded legal limits.

The state and the media could no longer ignore the evidence. LeeAnne testified before Congress about her family's experience, and public pressure mounted. The state was forced to change the way Flint's water was sourced and collected.

In 2018, LeeAnne won the Goldman Environmental Prize for blowing the whistle on the city of Flint. She had gone from a concerned mother to a grassroots citizen scientist, and she had learned more than how to test tap water—she'd learned how to gather the evidence that forces people to take you seriously. "Document everything," she advises other activists. "Even if it seems insignificant, keep track of it. Keep a timeline. Keep pictures. Get as much information as you can."

Information was one of LeeAnne's two most powerful tools—the other was her gut. "If you know something is wrong, follow your gut," she said. "You can make a difference even if you're going against some pretty big enemies."

REMEMBER TO RECHARGE

LeeAnne's battle to expose Flint's water problems was tough. Sometimes she needed to step away to rest, reflect, and recharge. "I cannot stress this enough," she said, "it is not only okay to take care of yourself, it is *necessary* for the longevity of the fight." Sometimes, she closes up social media and spends time with her loved ones until she has regained her "fighting spirit." LeeAnne is not alone. Many of the other activists in this book have talked about how they manage stress. Betty Kwan Chinn meditates every morning. Amythest Schaber makes time for personal interests, like comic books and cats. LaDonna Redmond says, "I highly recommend turning off the news and spending time in nature."

Marley Dias

STORIES MEAN MORE THAN STATISTICS

Marley Dias was 10 years old when, over pancakes at a diner near their home in New Jersey, her mother asked her a simple question, "If you could change one thing in the next year, what would it be?" Marley gave the question some thought. She had one pretty big complaint: She loved to read, but all the books she and her classmates read at school were about "white boys and their dogs." Marley wanted to read books about smart, strong black girls—girls like her.

With her mother's help, Marley got to work. Within a year, her social media campaign, #1000BlackGirlBooks, had collected almost 8,000 books featuring black girls as main characters. And her own school had replaced *Hatchet* and *Old Yeller* (books about white boys) with *One Crazy Summer* as required reading for all fourth graders. The book, by Rita Williams-Garcia, is about three black sisters who visit their mother in California in 1968. It became one of Marley's favorite books. (Another favorite book of Marley's is *Brown Girl Dreaming*, by Jacqueline Woodson. It's about a young girl growing up in New York and in racially segregated South Carolina as the civil rights movement grows in the 1960s and 1970s.)

Marley's goal with #1000BlackGirlBooks was simple yet enormous. She wanted to effect systemic—or deeply rooted and widespread—change. She could have chosen to focus on herself, to collect more "black girl books" and talk up her favorites to friends and teachers. Or she could have contacted authors and publishers and asked them to write and publish more books about black girls. But Marley went even further. She decided to start a social media campaign to collect black girl books, donate those books to schools and communities, develop a guide to the books so people could easily find them, and talk to legislators and teachers about making school reading lists more diverse.

If this wasn't a long enough to-do list, she also challenged herself to tell her own story. Marley's first book, *Marley Dias Gets It Done: And So Can You!*, was published by Scholastic when she was 13. It's a how-to guide for kids who want to make change and the adults who want to support them. And it's the kind of book that's all too rare in schools and community libraries—a story about a black girl by a black girl.

In her book, Marley shares nuggets of wisdom gleaned from her own experience as an activist. For example, she explains that stories are more powerful than numbers. Every budding activist should have a 60-second story ready to tell at any time, she says. Ask yourself: What happened in your life, your school, your community that frustrated you and made you want to make a change? That's your story.

WHAT'S AN ELEVATOR PITCH?

Marley is not the only one who knows the power of a short, persuasive story. Many people call this an *elevator pitch*. Imagine you are in an elevator with a VIP who could help your cause (or fund your business or get your movie made). You aren't exactly sure which floor your VIP is getting off on. In the short time you have to capture their attention and impress them with your ideas, what do you say? Practice your elevator pitch so you can sound confident and natural when you say it. Marley smartly suggests using your phone to record yourself reciting your pitch and to time your speech. Make sure it's short and compelling!

In Marley's 60-second story, she recounts how she told her mom about the lack of diversity in her class's books over pancakes. But really her story is much bigger. It's about not seeing herself reflected in the books she reads and wanting all kids to see themselves reflected in books. And Marley's story is far from finished. Next, she and her team, including her parents, plan to collect and distribute *one million* black girl books to libraries, schools, and communities throughout the world. They're working on an app to pair with a resource guide that will connect readers with books, and they're expanding their Black Girl Book Club for other after-school and summer programs.

Marley found her path to change by examining her love of reading and asking how she could love it even more. Passion is a key to success, as Marley says in her book. She urges young activists to choose subjects that will keep them going, "because you'll feel so much more joy in the things that you do."

"FRUSTRATION IS FUEL THAT CAN LEAD TO THE DEVELOPMENT OF AN INNOVATIVE AND USEFUL IDEA."

Lizzie Velasquez

STAND UP TO BULLIES

When Lizzie Velasquez was 17 years old and getting ready to go to college, she stumbled across a viral video on the Internet. The video was titled "The World's Ugliest Woman," and it had been watched more than four million times. The woman shown in the video was Lizzie herself.

The hateful viewer comments on the video were even more upsetting than the cruel title. "Each comment I read, I felt like someone was physically putting their fist through the screen and punching me," said Lizzie. Her life changed forever that day, but it changed for the better.

"If I could go back," said Lizzie, "I would tell myself, 'This is going to be the best thing that has ever happened to you.'" Lizzie has a genetic condition so rare that only two other people in the world share it. It's called neonatal progeroid syndrome, and it means that she can't gain weight and she's blind in one eye. Lizzie has never weighed more than 64 pounds. As a young girl growing up in Austin, Texas, Lizzie was surrounded by her supportive and loving family. She didn't realize she was different until her first day of kindergarten, when kids who didn't know her reacted with fear and disgust. Since then, Lizzie has been the victim of all kinds of bullying.

After she found the viral video of herself, Lizzie didn't think she'd ever feel better. So she made what she calls a "Love Yourself List." On the list, she wrote down everything she liked about herself. There was plenty. She's a caring person and a great listener, she loves to laugh, she really likes her hair, and more. She read her list over and over.

During high school, Lizzie taught herself how to be more outgoing. She joined clubs and the cheerleading squad and made friends with whom she could be herself. The confidence she forged back then continued through college, when she started to spread her message of self-acceptance by making inspirational videos and delivering motivational speeches.

By the time she graduated from college, Lizzie had written two books. She then gave a TEDx Talk called "How Do You Define Yourself?" In it, she uses humor and her own story to explain how to reject hateful feedback and accept and love yourself. That video went viral, and by early 2019, at age 30, Lizzie had more than two million followers on social media. A documentary about her life, *A Brave Heart: The Lizzie Velasquez Story*, debuted internationally in 2016. She also hosted an online interview series where she helped guests develop positive self-image using the power of fashion. Lizzie uses her motivational speeches, her Internet videos, and her books to spread her message far and wide. "You are the one who decides what defines you," says Lizzie. In her videos and talks, she warns against comparing yourself to others and letting magazines and television determine whether you think you're beautiful or valuable.

But before she could truly love herself and become an advocate for self-acceptance, Lizzie had to do something that many people find strange: She had to forgive the person who put up the video and the people who wrote the

FIND YOUR VOICE

"The most important lesson I've learned as an activist," said Lizzie, "is the power of one person's voice." She believes it comes in three steps. First, people need to decide what's really important to them. Then they need to speak up and fight for their beliefs or their cause. For Lizzie, the third step is crucial. After finding and learning to use your voice, "it's your turn to lend a hand to help someone else find their voice."

unkind comments. "You never know what these people are going through that are saying things to you and why—the reason behind it," she said.

Having compassion for the bully as well as the victim makes Lizzie's message even more powerful. "The victim is being hurt by the bully, and the bully is being hurt by someone or something that's going on in their lives," she said. "And if we're just tending to the victim and looking down at the bully, we're not really going to accomplish anything."

Lizzie has two main pieces of advice for anyone who's thinking about posting something online. First, remember that the Internet is written in pen, not pencil. "You can't just erase it and make it go away. It's always going to be there." And second, write down anything you want to put online, and picture yourself saying it to someone directly, face-to-face. "If you don't think you could tell what you're writing to someone else to their face, you should reword it or rethink what you were going to post."

"WHAT ARE YOUR BELIEFS, VALUES, AND PASSIONS? ONCE YOU'VE FOUND YOUR VOICE, IT'S TIME TO USE IT FOR GOOD."

Lizzie knows that despite her efforts, cyberbullying will never disappear. But there's a bright side. "It only takes one person to stand up for someone else online." And each of us has the power to be that person.

Billie Jean King

TRUST YOUR **INNER STRENGTH** (AND DEMAND EQUAL PAY!)

On September 20, 1973, Billie Jean King entered the Houston Astrodome on a reclining chair carried by a group of men dressed as ancient Egyptian slaves. Her opponent, former tennis champ Bobby Riggs, rode in on a rickshaw surrounded by beautiful women. Some 30,000 spectators were there in the stands—the largest crowd ever to attend a tennis match at the time. Millions more watched the game live on television. The event was billed as "the Battle of the Sexes."

The lead-up to the epic match looked like a ridiculous spectacle. At the time, Billie Jean was 29 years old. She'd won Wimbledon, a prestigious tennis tournament, five times. And for her, winning the game against 55-year-old Bobby was serious business. Four months earlier, Bobby had defeated another female Wimbledon champion, Margaret Court, in a match later called the "Mother's Day Massacre." Title IX, an act prohibiting sex discrimination in education (including school sports) had passed only one year before. Billie Jean—who began playing tennis after realizing that her first loves, basketball and baseball, weren't open to women—had testified before Congress on behalf of the law.

At the time, many women were hearing more and more about the new wave of feminism that had started in the 1960s. But they still weren't experiencing greater gender equality in their own lives or seeing it with their own eyes. Billie Jean had just founded the Women's Tennis Association to push for equal pay, because female players typically earned far less than men. Against that backdrop, Billie Jean knew she *had* to deliver on the court that day. "So much was going on to make women feel things were changing in the world. But in their own lives, not much had changed. There was a disconnect," she said. "That's what made this match huge."

A tennis player famous for thriving under pressure (one of her favorite sayings is "Pressure is a privilege"), Billie Jean ended up beating Bobby easily. She ran him ragged while she steadily blasted power shots from the baseline. It was a glorious display of athletic prowess—a woman unabashedly showing off her strength and endurance. The cultural significance of her victory was enormous. It helped earn female athletes everywhere a new kind of respect. "I wanted to help the women's movement, and it did," she said. "I wanted to help men and women understand each other better. And they did."

Billie Jean admits that she sometimes still wakes up in a cold sweat after dreaming that she hasn't played the match. But then she remembers that she *did* win—and breathes a giant sigh of relief. Not everyone was excited about her victory. She heard about one guy who was so mad after the match that he hurled his TV out of his window. But people still stop her on the street almost every day, she says, to tell her they remember gathering in the living room with their families and friends to watch the match. They tell her how thrilling it was to see her embody her message of gender equality by winning the battle.

Since then, Billie Jean, now an openly gay woman, has championed many other causes. She has fought for LGBTQ rights and racial justice. And she tries to help young girls, who quit playing sports at more than twice the rate of boys, stay involved with the games and competitions they love. In 2014, she launched the Billie Jean King Leadership Initiative, an organization dedicated to helping create diverse, inclusive workplaces where all people feel seen and respected. And she encourages people who might be nervous about breaking new ground and taking on big challenges, in any setting, with wisdom she's picked up playing tennis: "There's a time when you think you can't take another step, you can't continue, and there's some reserve you find in your body, in your soul that you didn't know you had," she once said in an interview. "You find it and . . . it allows you to rise to the occasion. Never underestimate the human spirit. *Never.*"

"EVERYONE IS AN INFLUENCER. I THINK SOMETIMES YOU FORGET THAT—FOR YOURSELF, FOR YOUR FAMILY, AND FOR THE WORLD. YOU CAN MAKE A DIFFERENCE."

Betty Kwan Chinn

INSPIRE THE COMMUNITY TO JOIN YOUR CAUSE

"**I** don't sleep a lot," says Betty Kwan Chinn, who wakes up at 2:07 a.m. every day. First, she makes enough breakfast and coffee to feed dozens of people, and then she drives to 11 different locations to deliver the food to the homeless. In the afternoon, she does it all over again for the dinner shift. "I forge a personal connection with [the homeless]," Betty said. "And then I ask them what they need, how can I help them." She says that she treats the people she meets—people struggling with mental illness or addiction and other people who are "just out of luck"—like they are family.

By the time Betty goes to bed, she has personally fed hundreds of homeless people in Humboldt County, California, where she lives. She does this because she doesn't want people to feel the hunger and isolation she felt when she was a child. When she was young, she was separated from her family by the Chinese government and forced to live on the streets. At the time, there was something called the Cultural Revolution happening in China, and the government was torturing and persecuting families like Betty's because of their wealth and religious beliefs. "I had nothing to eat," she recalls. She was forced to wear a sign around her neck that read "Child of the Devil."

After four years, Betty fled. She and three of her siblings hiked hundreds of miles and swam across the Pearl River to get to Hong

Kong. Betty had been so traumatized by living on the streets that she couldn't speak. She never went to school. Eventually, Betty found her way to the United States, where she married a university professor and had two sons. Though her new life was comfortable, she says she never forgot what it was like to go without food and shelter.

Then when her older son was in kindergarten, Betty found out that one of his classmates was a homeless girl. "She always stared at my son's lunch pail, and my son always gave her something to eat. I felt like I could do something. I can cook. So that's how I started," said Betty. Feeding one homeless girl turned into feeding a few families. Soon she was feeding hundreds of homeless people every day.

In 2008, Betty's homegrown operation got a big boost when, because of word of mouth in the community, she was awarded a grant of $25,000 from the California government. The prize, called the Minerva Award, is given to women who help others. With this money, as well as donations from private citizens and businesses, Betty partnered with St. Vincent de Paul, a local charity, to build showers and changing rooms for the homeless. The award also brought a lot of press. Soon Betty found herself the recipient of support and donations from individuals and organizations in the community. She formed a nonprofit agency and built three homeless shelters, including one just for families. People live in her shelters rent-free and receive three meals a day. Over the course of six to nine months, many are able to find jobs and rent apartments elsewhere.

Betty also opened a center where people can get job training and other support to find paths out of homelessness.

Betty believes that she's able to feed and shelter so many people only because of the acts of kindness performed by neighbors, friends, and strangers. Back when she started, she

The Village

didn't have a food truck or a license to distribute food, which got her into trouble with the police. So a friend raised money for her to buy a truck, which enabled her to get the license she needed. In 2018, her food truck was destroyed in an accident (Betty escaped with minor injuries). Members of the community posted about Betty's plight on Facebook and raised money to buy her a new truck. When Betty was building one of her shelters, a construction supplies company provided materials at cost (which means the company made no profit). Students have been a big help too! A Humboldt State University class did the work of figuring out how much it would cost to install a solar-powered water system. Betty's shelters also receive donations of clothing and food from drives organized by a local Boy Scout Troop, radio station, grocery co-op, and many nearby schools. "Betty is a magnet," said Russ Shaddix, a board member of St. Vincent de Paul. "People who don't support nonprofits—and I mean any nonprofits—do support Betty. She's just a magnet for support because of her personal commitment."

> **"EACH DAY IS A NEW DAY FOR ME, A NEW BEGINNING FOR ME. AND WHEN I FEED SOMEBODY, I FULFILL MYSELF."**

That said, some locals think that by feeding and clothing the homeless, Betty is actually encouraging homeless people to stay nearby. Sometimes, people shoot BB guns at Betty when she's making her rounds. Other people yell insults from their cars as they drive by. It's the insults, more than the BBs, that Betty minds the most.

Betty's goal isn't to end homelessness entirely. She admits that's not going to happen, but she wants to give people the tools they need to change their own lives. She also believes that by helping the homeless, she has come a long way in healing her own suffering. "I still carry my past every day. In a way, I'm healing myself."

Lady Gaga

RAISE **AWARENESS**—IN MUSIC, IN FASHION, AND WITH YOUR ACTIONS

Back in high school, Stefani Joanne Angelina Germanotta was not a superstar. "I was never the winner," she says now. "I was always the loser. And that still stays with me. And do I want to stick it to anybody? No. I just want to make music."

That's exactly what she does. Using her stage name, Lady Gaga, she has sold more than 11 million albums in the United States alone. She has performed at the Oscars and the Super Bowl and won numerous awards for her music and her acting. But she did not leave Stefani behind to become Lady Gaga. "I really make absolutely no separation between Stefani and Gaga," she has explained. She doesn't separate her work as an artist from her work as an activist either. She says she has always been an activist for causes she felt connected to, from marriage equality to mental health to opposing bullying. Of her audiences, she says, "I feel their stories. I listen to them. I meet with them. I see them. They write me letters—I read them. I'm in tune with what people want to change in the world."

One way Lady Gaga advocates for change is through her music. Her 2011 song "Born This Way" encouraged people of all races and sexual orientations to embrace their identities. Not everyone appreciated the message. Some broadcasters in Malaysia and the

United Kingdom cut the lyric "no matter gay, straight, or bi, lesbian, transgendered life, I'm on the right track, baby." Other broadcasters have asked her to edit her videos. Lady Gaga's response to these requests? "I say, 'Well, just tell them I won't do it, and if they don't want to play it, they don't have to.' That's it."

There have been times when even this superstar felt dispirited. At one point, she wanted to leave the music business. After spending days taking selfies or doing perfume promotions, she had to remind herself that she had more to offer as an artist than just an image. "Slowly but surely, I remembered who I am," Lady Gaga later said about that period of her career. "And then you go home, and you look in the mirror and you're like 'Yes, I can go to bed with you every night. . . . That person has integrity. That person has an opinion. That person just doesn't say yes.'"

So she has learned to say no. "As a woman in pop music," she promised the audience at an October 2009 gay rights rally in Washington, DC, "as a woman with the most beautiful gay fans in the whole world, to do my part, I refuse to accept any misogynistic and

WEAR YOUR STATEMENT

Lady Gaga was one of many activists who called attention to the military's "don't ask, don't tell" policy (which required gay and lesbian service members to hide their orientation or be discharged from the military). In September 2010, she showed up to the Video Music Awards in a dress made of meat. "If we don't stand up for what we believe in," she later explained, "if we don't fight for our rights, pretty soon we're going to have as much rights as the meat on our bones." The policy was repealed in December 2010. No one knows exactly how much Lady Gaga's meat dress affected the decision. But her choice to wear it certainly got people talking.

Another activist who has used fashion to get people talking about a cause is Marina DeBris. She makes incredible sculptures and dresses out of trash that has washed up on beaches to raise awareness about pollution and make people think twice before choosing single-use plastic items. She calls her wearable creations "trashion."

homophobic behavior in music, lyrics, or actions in the music industry."

In 2012, Lady Gaga and her mother, Cynthia Germanotta, created the Born This Way Foundation (BTWF), which builds and supports programs like #HackHarrassment, Channel Kindness, and #KindMonsters to raise awareness and combat bullying and harassment. BTWF also launched the Born Brave Bus Tour as a mobile safe space for fans—often known affectionately as "Little Monsters"—to talk about mental health and bullying, inspire self-acceptance and bravery, and connect with mental health resources. One of BTWF's most recent campaigns was a partnership with the National Council for Behavioral Health in 2018 for the #BeKindBeTheDifference campaign. The campaign encourages people to learn how to respond to signs of mental illness or substance abuse.

Lady Gaga still seeks out new ways to use her powerful voice, her art, and her experiences as a bullied teen to shine a spotlight on the people who are struggling. "When I was 22," she told NPR (National Public Radio) in 2016, "putting out my first couple records, I was a baby—and nobody really views you as any type of role model or anything. But as you get older, you realize that you have the attention of a lot of young people. And you think, 'Okay, well, what should I say now? What can I say that will be impactful in a positive way?'"

"JUST BE KIND. THE ACT ITSELF IS FREE. AND IT'S PRICELESS."

Emma González

FIND YOUR ALLIES—AND GIVE POLITICIANS
A PIECE OF YOUR MIND

Emma González said that taking swift and strong action to protest weak gun laws was her way to grieve. On February 14, 2018, a young man with a gun entered Marjory Stoneman Douglas (MSD) High School in Parkland, Florida, and killed 17 students and staff members. Emma was an 18-year-old senior at the school. Three days after the tragedy, she stepped up to the mic at a rally outside the federal courthouse in Fort Lauderdale, and her words moved the crowd. "The people in the government who were voted into power are lying to us. And us kids seem to be the only ones who notice and are prepared to call B.S.," Emma shouted. "They say that tougher gun laws do not decrease gun violence—we call B.S.!" she continued, with the crowd joining in to echo her. "They say a good guy with a gun stops a bad guy with a gun—we call B.S.! . . . They say that no laws could have been able to prevent the hundreds of senseless tragedies that have occurred—we call B.S.! That us kids don't know what we're talking about, that we're too young to understand how the government works—we call B.S.!"

Emma wiped her eyes and ended with a request: register to vote and give elected officials "a piece of your mind!" Videos of the speech went viral. Emma became a household name. And along with some

MSD classmates, she founded the Never Again movement—a new generation of tech-smart, media-savvy students fighting for stricter gun safety laws.

Emma is a bright student who took full advantage of her public school's rich array of classes and clubs. She certainly knew how to craft a persuasive argument (she'd recently made a PowerPoint presentation that convinced her parents to let her shave her head). She and her fellow activists used every tool they could think of: speaking to the press, marching, sharing on social media platforms like Twitter, and even going on a bus tour and giving speeches at rallies. Emma touched people by describing honestly what it was like to lose longtime school friends and take on this difficult fight.

A DIGITAL MEGAPHONE

Emma said she'd never used Twitter before the shooting, but she quickly mastered the platform and used it to spread her message far and wide. In her tweets, she called out the hypocrisy of politicians who offer sympathy for shooting victims but also take hefty campaign contributions from the National Rifle Association (NRA), a powerful group dedicated to blocking tighter gun safety laws. Her comments were quickly retweeted. She also noted on Twitter and elsewhere that Donald Trump had received millions of dollars in support from the NRA during his presidential campaign. Two weeks after the shooting, Emma had gained more than 955,000 followers, while the NRA, which had been on Twitter since 2009, had only 584,000.

Sitting cross-legged on the couch during an appearance on *The Ellen DeGeneres Show,* Emma talked about her viral speech at the courthouse rally. She explained how she'd hit upon her unforgettable refrain, "We call B.S." (which is now a staple on protest buttons and signs). "I knew that I would get my job done properly at that rally if I got people chanting something. And I thought 'We call B.S.' has four syllables—that's good, I'll use that," she said. "I didn't want to say the actual curse words . . . this message doesn't need to be thought of in a negative way."

On March 24, 2018, Emma and other student activists from Parkland led the March for Our Lives, an event that drew hundreds of thousands of protesters to Washington, DC, and sparked more than 800 related events (including school walkouts) across the country (and around the world!). After she finished high school in June, Emma spent her summer vacation on a bus tour called the March for Our Lives: Road to Change. The tour went to cities, such as Chicago, Houston, and Milwaukee, where gun violence is far more common than it is in Parkland. The group registered thousands of new voters and met with hundreds of other young gun-violence survivors from all walks of life. They talked, collaborated, and strategized—and shared plenty of hugs and laughs too.

Emma came away from the tour having met "so many beautiful people," and she wrote on Twitter that she "learned about too many who have been lost to gun violence." But the tour—one of "the most impactful experiences of my life"—also left her feeling very optimistic about her generation's chances of finally pushing politicians to enact stricter gun laws. "The future of America is brighter than it's been in a long time," she wrote. "I have hope."

> "THIS COUNTRY'S GOVERNMENT WAS MADE TO WORK SLOWLY, BUT IF WE ELECT THE RIGHT PEOPLE AND KEEP MOVING AS FAST AS WE HAVE BEEN, **WE WILL CHANGE OUR WORLD FOR THE BETTER.**"

Rachel Carson

SHOW READERS WHAT'S **AT STAKE**

More than any other book before it, Rachel Carson's *Silent Spring* helped people think about how their day-to-day actions impact the planet. Rachel wrote the book shortly after World War II, when Americans were newly aware of the harmful effects of the radiation spread by atomic bombs. She explained how spraying pesticide chemicals over backyards and crops could be dangerous too. *Silent Spring* became an instant best seller when it was first published in 1962. It launched the modern environmental movement.

Born in western Pennsylvania in 1907, Rachel grew up roaming her family's farm. Her mother taught her the names of the plants and the calls of the birds living there. Rachel became a careful observer of nature's details, with a gift for describing what she found. She said she always knew she'd become a writer. In a story she wrote as a teenager, she described "the frame-work of sticks which the cuckoo calls a nest, and the lichen-covered home of the humming-bird."

After studying marine biology in college and earning a master's degree in zoology from Johns Hopkins University, Rachel went to work analyzing data and writing pamphlets for the US Bureau of Fisheries (later the US Fish and Wildlife Service). She was the only member of her family earning a salary during the Great Depression. To help support her widowed mother and two nieces, she also wrote newspaper and magazine articles on marine life. The articles' success led her to write *Under the Sea-Wind*, about the lives of fish and seabirds. Later, she published two popular books about the world's oceans, *The Sea Around Us* (1951) and *The Edge of the Sea* (1955).

Finally, Rachel returned to writing about land and its inhabitants with passion and concern. Reading government wildlife reports, she'd learned about new dangers to the ecosystem posed by a chemical pesticide called DDT. The military used DDT to kill lice during the war, and it was first sold to farmers and gardeners in 1945. But no one had tested its safety in such everyday settings. Soon there were reports of birds, fish, and other animals dying in areas where DDT had been sprayed.

In *Silent Spring*, Rachel wrote with a combination of scientific insight and poetic detail. She showed how upsetting one part of nature can cause more harm down the line. She wrote, "We spray our elms, and the following springs are silent of robin song, not because we sprayed the robins directly but because the poison traveled, step by step, through the now familiar elm leaf–earthworm–robin cycle." Rachel explained that these effects were observable and recordable. She wrote, "They reflect the web of life—or death—that scientists know as ecology."

"THE MORE CLEARLY WE CAN FOCUS OUR ATTENTION ON THE WONDERS AND REALITIES OF THE UNIVERSE ABOUT US, THE LESS TASTE WE SHALL HAVE FOR THE DESTRUCTION OF OUR RACE."

Three months after reading portions of *Silent Spring* in the *New Yorker* magazine, President John F. Kennedy created a commission to explore the long-lasting toxic effects of pesticides. Unfortunately, Rachel died of breast cancer in 1964. She didn't live long enough to see all of the environmental regulations her book prompted, including the Clean Water Act (1972) and the Endangered Species Act (1973). She also missed the founding of the Environmental Protection Agency in 1970. That, too, was a direct result of her work.

Christie Begnell

YOUR CREATIVITY CAN **HELP** YOU—AND OTHERS TOO

Artist and author Christie Begnell has created a monster. In her drawings, Ana is a looming, skeletal woman with blank yellow eyes and skin the color of a bruise. She's a creature that told her she was fat, worthless, disgusting. Ana represents Christie's eating disorder. Christie began drawing Ana and other images while in treatment. It was a way to deal with her emotions and to show her mother what was going on with her. Ana was also a way to separate the healthy Christie from the disordered Christie. "On days when I was feeling defeated," she said, "I'd draw Ana sitting on a throne with a crown on her head. On days I felt strong, I'd draw her lying on the ground beneath me." Soon drawing was part of Christie's recovery.

But Christie's artwork is not only self-expression. It's also her chosen form of activism. "I illustrate the realities of eating disorders as traumatic mental illnesses with the capability of destroying lives to fight the idea that they are a phase young white girls go through in order to receive attention," she explains. "My wish for my work is that the world becomes educated about eating disorders and that those who are suffering don't have to feel ashamed to reach out for help."

In addition to publishing her artwork online and in books, Christie found another way to counter harmful messages. On Instagram, where her account @meandmyed.art has more than 34,000 followers, she points out that men can have eating disorders, too, and that a person who appears to be at a healthy weight can still have a dangerous illness. She creates drawings showing healthy and powerful bodies of all colors, shapes, and sizes. She offers advice and support to people struggling with eating disorders. Christie also joined the body positive (BoPo) movement, where she found accounts, like @bodyposipanda, that have helped her feel confident and hopeful.

Christie admires powerful women like Lady Gaga, Demi Lovato, and Kesha for fighting to change the way the world views mental illness. "They showed me that you could talk openly about eating disorders, addiction, and trauma, and still be respected and loved," she explains.

Christie is now working toward becoming a psychologist, specializing in eating disorders. One recent challenge for her has been accepting the body changes that came with her first pregnancy. "A woman's body is a magnificent thing," Christie says. "There's so much power in it—we can even carry life within us! But we're constantly told by society that we have to be skinny. I just think, 'No! What about what a body can actually do?'"

"**I TRULY BELIEVE THAT IF YOU CAN MAKE A DIFFERENCE IN ONE PERSON'S LIFE, YOU HAVE DONE AN AMAZING JOB, AND WHEN IT COMES TO ISSUES LIKE MENTAL HEALTH, YOU'RE POTENTIALLY SAVING A LIFE.**"

A NEW PERSPECTIVE

One of Christie's most popular drawings is her "I feel fat" translation wheel. "I hope it shows people that when they say they 'feel fat,' there's an emotion underneath, and it's important to find out what that emotion is." The translation wheel suggests a range of emotions, including overwhelmed, jealous, lonely, and ashamed. Christie says, "People have told me it's helped them think in a different way."

Jasilyn Charger

FIND A NEW SENSE OF **PURPOSE**

Sometimes getting involved in political activism has positive effects that are both public and personal. It not only shines light on a critical issue, but it also helps the people fighting for truth and justice find powerful new meaning in their lives.

Both things happened when Jasilyn Charger, a 19-year-old Lakota Sioux born on the Cheyenne River Reservation in South Dakota, became a youth leader. She helped rally teens from her reservation and others nearby to fight for the protection of clean water and save their sacred tribal lands.

Many Native Americans live in areas where poverty is widespread. And Jasilyn is no exception. Her home county is one of the poorest in the country. Like many Native Americans living in communities where hope is often hard to find, she had already seen friends, relatives, and neighbors struggling with post-traumatic stress disorder (PTSD), addiction, and even suicide.

A few years earlier, she'd gotten into trouble herself. Sometimes, she'd leave town on weekends to go looking for odd jobs to help her family pay their bills. After leaving home too many times, she was sent to a group home, where she fell out of touch with her beloved twin sister, Jasilea. She fell into a deep depression. When she aged out of the group home at 17, she started to use drugs herself.

Fortunately, one of Jasilyn's brothers spoke up and got her to stop. "He woke me up. He saw that I was hurting myself, and he told me it was enough—that I was a woman, I was a Lakota woman. There's a moment when I faced my dragon, and I won. That was the first battle I ever won."

After she got sober, Jasilyn started tagging along with her brother and other politically active friends when they went to protest events. She heard about a company's plans to construct the Dakota Access Pipeline, an oil-transport pipeline that would span more than 1,000 miles. The pipeline would travel under the Missouri River, which provides drinking water to the nearby Standing Rock Sioux Reservation, as well as other reservations downstream. People in the area worried that the pipeline could jeopardize the safety of their drinking water. In April 2016, she hurried up to Standing Rock, where a handful of others were setting up a protest "prayer camp" near the pipeline's proposed route.

The Standing Rock protest began as a small, hardscrabble operation. But Jasilyn and other youth leaders found creative ways to draw attention to their cause. In July 2016, Jasilyn helped to organize a run, all the way from North Dakota, where their camp was set up, to Washington, DC. She even ran in the race. Passing through her hometown, she literally ran through her old house, waking up Jasilea and getting her to come along as a rider in the support van. The sisters grew close again as they realized how deeply they cared about protecting their tribe's sacred land.

A STRONG TRADITION

Jasilyn comes from a long line of incredible Native American women activists. Lyda Conley, of the Wyandot Nation, stood guard with a musket over a sacred burial ground that had been sold to the US government in 1906. Eventually, she became the first Native American woman to argue a case before the Supreme Court. Writer and activist Gertrude Simmons, known as Zitkala-Sa, founded the National Council of American Indians to advocate for Native rights. Wilma Mankiller changed the lives of many of her fellow Cherokees when she organized community self-help projects to fix dangerous housing conditions and build a modern water system for a community in Oklahoma. She became the first woman principal chief of the Cherokee Nation.

Meanwhile, more and more tepees and tents continued to pop up at the camp. And over the next few months, the Standing Rock protest united thousands of unexpected political allies—rural farmers, urban environmentalists, older tribal leaders, as well as hundreds of other Native American teens—around their shared opposition to the pipeline.

In December of 2016, Jasilyn and her fellow water protectors won a big victory when plans for the Dakota Access Pipeline were put on hold. Its engineers were ordered to seek a new route for the pipeline. But the victory was short-lived. Donald Trump took office in 2017. One of his first actions was to sign executive orders allowing the Dakota Access Pipeline and the Keystone XL pipeline (another pending oil pipeline that protesters continue to fight) to proceed. Despite this disappointment, Jasilyn says she's never going to stop fighting to protect herself and the safety and well-being of others in her community and the generations of Sioux yet to come.

As she said in 2018, camping at Standing Rock "really connected me through not only spirituality, not only fighting for what I thought was right, but combining the two. Activism and spirituality live hand in hand . . . and for me it was just the starting point of the road that has become my life." Looking back, she wishes she'd been more open to help when she began fighting for her cause. But she reminds other activists: "No matter where you are in the world, there is someone who wants to help. If your plea falls on deaf ears, it will echo and find open hearts."

"IT'S OKAY TO BE AFRAID. BUT HAVE COURAGE TO MOVE PAST YOUR FEAR AND DEMAND BETTER NOT ONLY FOR YOUR GENERATION BUT FOR GENERATIONS TO COME."

Jane Goodall

DARE TO **DREAM** AND **ACT**

Growing up in England during World War II, Jane Goodall saved up to buy herself a secondhand book. She climbed into her favorite tree and read the treasured book—*Tarzan of the Apes*, the story of a man raised by apes in Africa—cover to cover. And by the time she finished, Jane had dreamed up a life plan: she wanted to live in Africa "with wild animals and write books about them," she recalled at 83.

People laughed and told her it would never happen because she was just a girl, and girls can't do things like that. But even though her family was poor, Jane's mother, Vanne, never laughed at her dream. Instead Vanne told her, "If you never give up, you'll find a way."

Vanne was right. By working as a waitress and saving up her wages, Jane was able to visit a friend who lived in Kenya. There she met the world-famous anthropologist Louis Leakey. (Anthropologists are scientists who study human beings and their behavior and interactions throughout time.) Based in Kenya, Leakey was exploring the evolution of the earliest human species in Africa. He saw that Jane's inherent curiosity and adventurousness made her well suited for work in the field. So, in 1960, he set her up at a camp in the Gombe Stream Game Reserve (now a national park in Tanzania). At the time, women were strongly discouraged from traveling alone, so she embarked, accompanied by her mother, on a project of observing and recording the behavior of chimpanzees. Because chimpanzees and humans share a common ancestor, they are considered to be closely related.

Wearing simple khaki shirts and shorts, Jane blended into the environment. She had the patience to wait—and wait—until the chimpanzees learned to accept her presence and go about their usual business. She observed the chimpanzees for nearly 30 years! And thanks to her groundbreaking research in Gombe, we now know that chimpanzees are omnivorous, which means they eat both meat and plants (previously people thought they ate only plants). Jane also found out that chimpanzees are capable of making and using tools, and that they are highly social creatures. Like humans, chimpanzees thrive in the company of other chimps they trust and have fun with.

Jane eventually earned a doctoral degree in ethology (the study of animal behavior) from Cambridge University. And after discovering a group of chimpanzees bopping and swaying near a waterfall, she even came to believe that they are capable of experiencing awe—being spiritually wowed by the beauty of nature, as we humans often are. Chimpanzees "can't analyze it, they don't talk about it, they can't describe what they feel," she explained. But watching them, "you get the feeling that it's all locked up inside them, and the only way they can express it is through this fantastic rhythmic dance."

Jane's great contribution to science is helping us understand that the sharp dividing line that people thought existed between animals and humans simply isn't there—instead, it's "a fuzzy line." And while humans and chimpanzees are unique, "we humans are just not as different as we used to think." Through her many best-selling books and fascinating television specials, Jane became famous and beloved for showing us how much we have in common with chimpanzees, who share nearly 99% of our DNA.

Because she's spent so much time watching and learning from chimpanzees, seeing the impacts of climate change in Africa has been particularly upsetting for Jane. So has seeing forests around the Gombe National Park disappear over the years as people have chopped down trees, either to make charcoal (which is produced by burning wood) or create more farmable land. Losing these surrounding forests has put endangered wild animals living in the reserve, like chimpanzees, under stress because they no longer have a buffer of land to forage in to find clean water or additional food. But both of these things have spurred her to use her scientific star power to draw attention to environmental issues and teach people about why we need to take better care of the land and climate we share with so many other marvelous animals.

Jane now spends most of her time working and traveling to promote forest conservation and environmental protection. But she's been most inspired, she says, by watching Roots & Shoots, a program she started in 1991, catch on with kids all around the world. The program encourages kids to dream up their own plans for helping animals and protecting the environment.

"THE WAY FORWARD, I THINK . . . IS TO FIND A BETTER WAY TO CONDUCT OURSELVES ON THIS PLANET."

"The planet has finite natural resources, and we're using them up as though they'll go on forever. . . . we're running out of fresh water. We're chopping up forests. We're losing animal species," she said. But while some adults give up hope, young people "get it. They realize it might be nothing to pick up a piece of plastic each day and recycle, to get organic food, and to be vegetarian. That moves us towards the kind of world we would all like to think we have."

Aiko Herzig-Yoshinaga

WORK TO HEAL
HISTORY'S WOUNDS

The word *camp* has a lot of different meanings. A *summer camp* is one thing, a *base camp* is another thing—and an *internment camp* is something else entirely.

When Aiko Herzig-Yoshinaga was 17 years old in Los Angeles, California, she loved the beach, was crazy about her boyfriend, and was looking forward to the prom. She probably didn't know what an internment camp was. But then she was forced into one by the US government, along with 120,000 other Japanese Americans.

The year was 1942, World War II was in full swing, and the Japanese military had just bombed a US naval base in Hawaii. Aiko's high school principal told her and her Japanese-American friends that they wouldn't finish high school. She recalled him saying, "You're not getting your diplomas because your people bombed Pearl Harbor."

Aiko and her boyfriend eloped so they could go to the same camp. Aiko's family was moved to a different camp. The internment camp was made up of bare, tar-papered rooms where several families were housed together. In the rooms were metal cots and a potbellied stove, and that was it. No kitchen, no bathroom, no closet or dresser or table. It was more like a prison. "The first day, we were given a big sack and told to go fill it up with hay. That was our mattress," said Aiko in an interview.

Aiko gave birth to her first child in the camp, though the medical facilities were poor and there was no fresh milk. After three years, she and her family were released.

For a while, Aiko didn't spend too much energy thinking about why the US government had done what it did. But then, in the 1960s and 1970s, when she was in her fifties, she joined some human rights and civil rights groups, including Asian Americans for Action, or AAA. Then she started spending a lot of time at the National Archives, in Washington, DC. The National Archives is an immense collection of the government's letters, memos, and photographs. It includes transcripts from important moments in US history, including the internment of Japanese Americans during World War II.

Aiko became a master archivist, which is a lot like being a detective—you have to examine every piece of evidence for clues. She came to believe that the government had lied about its reasons for putting Japanese Americans into camps. The government claimed the camps were necessary because the United States and Japan were at war, and there was no time to figure out who was an enemy of the state and who wasn't. According to the government, the whole thing was just an honest mistake. Aiko was determined to prove that this wasn't true.

And one day in 1982, after years of searching, Aiko lived every detective's dream when she came across a *smoking gun,* or a piece of evidence that can't be ignored. What she found was a red bound book that contained a secret report written by a military lieutenant.

"ALL YOU CAN DO IS KEEP FIGHTING. EVEN AS AN OLD LADY, I'M STILL JOINING CAUSES. AND IF MY FEET ALLOW ME, I'LL BE **MARCHING IN THE STREETS**."

Originally, there were 10 copies of the report, but the rest had been burned in an effort to protect the government's secret: the real reason for the internment camps was racism against Japanese Americans and hasty, hysterical political leadership.

For years, Aiko had been researching the United States's imprisonment of Japanese citizens. Her goal was to convince the government to accept responsibility and offer an apology. Now she'd found just the evidence she needed! She shared her discovery with the congressional group she worked for—the Commission on Wartime Relocation and Internment of Civilians. With Aiko's key evidence, the group convinced President Ronald Reagan to sign the Civil Liberties Act of 1988, which gave every living survivor of the camps $20,000 and an official apology. This was 47 years after Aiko was first imprisoned, an experience she had never tried to forget. In fact, she kept a coiled piece of barbed wire in her apartment, a reminder of the injustice and an emblem of her fight for change.

Aiko was rarely in front of cameras. She did not give speeches. But her work as an archivist changed the government's stance on the incarcerations. Hers was a quieter form of activism but activism nonetheless. Aiko never sought public recognition. She gave credit to a team of researchers and said she was privileged to be part of it.

Before her death in 2018 at the age of 93, Aiko was the subject of a documentary called *Rebel with a Cause*, and she donated her archive of 33,000 documents to the University of California. "I exhort you to go for it," she said about being an activist late in life. "Don't let age deter you!"

CHOOSE WORDS WISELY

During her years as an archivist, Aiko kept track of terms the government used to talk about the internment. These terms—including the word *internment*—were euphemisms. A euphemism is a polite, inoffensive word or phrase meant to paint a rosy picture over an ugly reality. The government used words like *relocation* and *evacuation*, but the honest words were *imprisonment*, *exile*, and *banishment*. In 2009, Aiko wrote an essay based on her findings, titled "Words Can Lie or Clarify."

Jazz Jennings

SHINE A LIGHT ON PEOPLE SOCIETY RARELY SEES

In Jazz Jennings's own words, she is "just a typical teen girl living my life . . . who happens to be transgender." She loves hanging out with her family and friends, playing soccer, and studying. Like many of her peers, she feels insecure and can be too hard on herself sometimes, she says. Yet unlike most teenage girls, Jazz also has a YouTube channel with more than 600,000 subscribers (and counting!). And she's on a mission to educate people about what it means to be assigned one sex at birth but identify with another gender, which is the definition of *transgender*. To get her message across, she uses YouTube; her reality show, *I Am Jazz;* and more. Just being herself in public is an important part of her activism. She gives people the chance to see what it's like to live as a transgender person. Viewers can see and relate to her as a regular person.

"Ever since I could form coherent thoughts, I knew I was a girl trapped inside a boy's body. There was never any confusion in my mind," she explained in her 2016 autobiography, *Being Jazz*. But the "confusing part," she noted, "was why no one else could see what was wrong." As soon as Jazz was able to communicate as a toddler, she began telling her parents that even though she had a boy's body, she knew she had a "girl brain." Her parents assumed that this and her love of dressing up in girls' clothes were part of a passing phase.

But once Jazz's mom and dad realized that Jazz's determination to live as a girl was not only persistent, but growing stronger over time, they consulted with doctors and other specialists in gender identity. They learned that people who aren't free to live according to their authentic gender identity often experience serious distress. They also learned that, because they feel bullied or rejected by members of their family or community, almost half of all transgender youth attempt suicide.

Starting in kindergarten, Jazz lived openly as a girl, leaving her hair long and wearing girls' clothing to school. Still, Jazz faced challenges at school that made her feel isolated and uncomfortable. Her school wouldn't let her use the girls' bathroom and requested that she use an unmarked bathroom in the school nurse's office instead. But one day, when Jazz was in second grade and had to pee badly, she snuck into the nearest girls' restroom. Unfortunately, a staff member found her there and got really upset, threatening to call Jazz's parents and the principal.

"It was terrible, and one of the first times I realized discrimination is present and I'm being treated differently for being transgender," Jazz has said of the incident. "I always considered myself to be like everyone else because I *am* like everyone else, but they didn't make me feel that way."

Right now, an evolving legal battle over transgender rights is being fought over access to school bathrooms and in other ways. Thousands of schools and businesses across the country have started providing gender-neutral

> **"WE NEED TO KEEP OUR FOCUS ON FOSTERING GROWTH AND BEING THE BEST WE CAN BE RATHER THAN DWELLING ON THOSE WHO TRY TO UNDERMINE OUR EXISTENCE."**

bathrooms for trans people and others who prefer not to identify with any specific gender identity. Others, however, are eager to strip back protections for transgender students and adults, so people who define themselves as transgender would no longer be allowed to serve in the military or receive certain guarantees for health care and other rights that transgender people have under current laws.

Jazz started taking hormones to stave off male adolescence before puberty. And in the summer of 2018, she had what's known as gender confirmation surgery—a medical procedure that altered her existing genitalia to resemble female genitalia. The surgery went well, she said in a quick vlog update she posted a few weeks later. She also said she'd share more about it on the next season of *I Am Jazz*, her TLC reality series. She and her family decided to participate in the show when she was 14, because she realized it was an opportunity to help transgender youth, who often aren't fully accepted in society, see their experience (or one like it) normalized on mainstream TV.

Putting honest, detailed, heartfelt information out there is important to Jazz and her family, so they can help other families with transgender children spark their own important conversations. Yet mostly, Jazz wants her own story to serve as a relatable road map for other transgender kids. It's easy to get discouraged. But Jazz reminds kids to look at the big picture. "I am 100% confident," she says, "that we will one day live in a world where everyone is free to be their authentic self, and we can live with peace, love, and harmony in our hearts." Her advice? "The key is to focus on the positive," she says.

SPEAK FROM THE HEART

While on the campaign trail, Donald Trump promised to support LGBTQ rights. But, as president, he began pushing for rollbacks to these rights. And if Jazz had the chance to sit down with the president, she says she'd "look in his eyes and say, 'You know, I'm here speaking on behalf of the transgender youth. Why do you have to treat us this way? We are just kids, and we just want to be happy, and we deserve to be treated equally and respected for who we are.'"

Sophie Cruz

GET YOUR **MESSAGE** INTO POWERFUL HANDS

Sophie Cruz was only five years old when she stepped across a parade barricade in Washington, DC, to deliver a letter to the pope. She had traveled from Los Angeles to see Pope Francis and request his help for the undocumented immigrants living in the United States. This group includes Sophie's parents, who moved to the United States illegally from Oaxaca, Mexico.

The government limits the number of people who can move to the United States legally, and there are many more people who want to live and work here than the government allows. Currently, about 11 million people live in the United States without permission or legal status. They are often called undocumented immigrants.

Because Sophie and her sister were born in America, they are American citizens. But Sophie and millions of other children share the fear that they will be separated from their families if their parents are deported, or sent back to their home country. This fear was what Sophie hoped to share with Pope Francis.

The first time Sophie tried to reach the pope as his vehicle passed by, she was stopped by security guards. The second time Sophie tried, Pope Francis motioned for her to come over. When security guards lifted her up for a hug and a blessing, she gave her letter to the pope. Sophie hoped he might read her letter and ask

President Obama to pass immigration reform so that families like hers would no longer live in constant fear of being broken apart. In the letter, she explained that she was sad and scared that her parents could be taken from her. She wrote, "My dad works very hard in a factory galvanizing pieces of metal. All immigrants just like my dad feed this country. They deserve to live with dignity."

Sophie was chosen for this job by a group of organizations called the Full Rights for Immigrants Coalition, but Sophie herself chose what she wanted to say. "She didn't have anyone coaching her," said Juan Jose Gutierrez, a member of the coalition. "She just spoke from her heart. It all came from her."

Sometimes an act as simple as writing and delivering a heartfelt letter can have a major impact. A lot of people saw the video of Sophie's encounter with the pope. She found herself in the national spotlight. President Obama invited her to the White House, and she is the subject of a documentary called *Free Like the Birds*. In 2018, El Mac (Miles MacGregor) painted a giant mural called *Sophie Holding the World Together* at the Children's Discovery Museum of San Jose. It shows Sophie holding a lotus flower in one hand and the Earth in the other.

Sophie continues to share her story and ask questions of the people who have the power to affect lives. In early 2017, at the Women's March in Washington, DC, Sophie delivered a speech before an estimated 470,000 people. She reminded children and families to hold on to their strength. "We are here together, making a chain of love to protect our families," she told the crowd.

> "LET US FIGHT WITH **LOVE, FAITH, AND COURAGE** SO THAT OUR FAMILIES WILL NOT BE DESTROYED."

Lidiya Yankovskaya

MAKE YOUR MESSAGE WITH **MUSIC**

In 2015, Russian-American conductor Lidiya Yankovskaya spent the summer traveling in Europe, where hundreds of thousands of Syrian refugees were seeking shelter after fleeing a civil war in their country. Lidiya noticed two things about the crisis. The first was that some countries, like Germany, welcomed the refugees. "Despite the fact that it literally was thousands of people just walking across the border—thousands . . . despite that, the Germans really welcomed the individuals coming in," Lidiya said in an interview. "Towns opened their homes and built shelters and found ways to help people get jobs." The second thing Lidiya noticed was that other countries, like the United States, were working actively to limit immigration. To Lidiya, the wave of protesters and politicians speaking out against immigration didn't seem like political policy—it seemed more like racism. "To me, it was clear that largely this was an issue that had to do with racism, that had to do with discrimination against Muslims," said Lidiya.

Lidiya knew about discrimination. She's Jewish and, when she was nine years old, she and her mother fled St. Petersburg, Russia, and came to the United States to escape a wave of anti-Semitism. Lidiya has vivid memories of Nazi demonstrations and pamphlets being circulated that urged violence against Jewish people.

Lidiya knew from experience that refugees were important members of society, but she wanted to show it. In December 2015, she announced on her Facebook page that she was organizing a refugee orchestra. She wanted to show people that many refugees are actively contributing to American culture and society. "When people hear the word *refugee*, they have an image in their heads of people on a boat or in a camp. These kind of preconceptions can cloud the fact that refugees are not only people like you and me—they can, and do, contribute enormous cultural value," said Lidiya.

The Refugee Orchestra Project made its debut in May 2016 in Cambridge, Massachusetts. Lidiya initially intended to give one concert, but the orchestra was so successful that she was immediately invited to do another, then another, and another. Over the next couple of years, the project re-formed in every city where it performed, including Boston, and Washington, DC. They even performed at the United Nations in New York City.

The Refugee Orchestra Project is Lidiya's way of giving back to the people who inspire her, including refugees like her mother. "There are so many wonderful people who want to be allies but just don't know how," said Lidiya. "As a leader of this type of organization, it's essential that I empower others to become part of the cause."

> **"SOMETIMES YOU FAIL—AND THAT'S OKAY. YOU SIMPLY CHANGE TACTICS, AND YOU TRY AGAIN. WITH ANY LUCK, YOU MAY HAVE PLANTED A SEED IN SOMEONE'S MIND THAT WILL GROW IN THE FUTURE."**

LEAD BY EXAMPLE

Lidiya started conducting back in high school, when her teacher and mentor asked her to give it a shot. She was a natural. When she was appointed music director of the Chicago Opera Theater, she became the only female music director of a major opera company in the United States—but she hopes that won't be true forever. "I hope girls and women will be emboldened to know they can make a career in my (still!) almost exclusively male profession," said Lidiya.

Malala Yousafzai

RAISE **YOUR** VOICE

In 2009, when she was just 11 years old, Malala Yousafzai began writing a blog about life in her home, the Swat Valley of Pakistan. The area was dominated by Taliban fighters. The Taliban—religious extremists who don't believe women should be educated—were shutting down schools and attempting to ban education for girls. But as the daughter of a local school owner, Malala devoured lessons in poetry, science, and foreign languages. She also spoke out in defense of every girl's right to receive an education and determine her future.

"They cannot stop me. I will get my education, if it is at home, school, or anyplace. This is our request to all the world: Save our schools. Save our world. Save our Pakistan. Save our Swat," she told a reporter. She hoped the reporter would help spread word about the humanitarian crisis in Pakistan.

In October 2012, in retaliation for Malala's activism, a Taliban gunman boarded her school bus and shot her in the head. She was airlifted to Birmingham, England, where doctors performed multiple surgeries to save her life. When she recovered, she remembered almost nothing of the shooting itself. Later, she told an interviewer she was surprised and thrilled to discover that she had inspired hundreds of thousands of people—not just in Pakistan but all over the world—to speak out about the injustice of denying girls education. "When I was attacked, many people stood up . . . against the extremists," she said, "not just the people but against the ideology. That's what we have to fight against—ideology that exists there that does not accept women as equal to men, that does not accept women to have the right to education." She wants to fight that ideology "whether it exists in the mountains of Pakistan, or . . . in the big cities, in New York, or in Washington, or anywhere."

Addressing the United Nations General Assembly in 2013, Malala earned a standing ovation for her speech. "The terrorists thought that they would change my aims and stop my ambitions, but nothing changed in my life except this: weakness, fear, and hopelessness died. Strength, power, and courage was born," she said. The following year, at age 17, she became the youngest person ever to receive the Nobel Peace Prize.

In her speeches and advocacy, Malala makes it clear that poverty, violence, and other problems stem from denying women the right to education and career opportunities equal to men's. The solution, she explains, is not complicated. She says, "Governments need to invest more money into education. Business people, everyone who is a part of society—they need to start thinking about investing in girls and their education. We just need an ambition and an intention. What you do is then easy."

Before setting off to start college at Oxford University in October 2017, Malala posted a funny question to her nearly one-million-strong band of Twitter followers: "Packing for university. Any tips? Advice? Dos and dont's? #HelpMalalaPack." Now she's settled into student life at Oxford. She loves college (and was happy to bring along flip-flops for the dorm shower, as one smart person on her Twitter feed advised her to do). Most of her time is devoted to studying for her classes in philosophy, politics, and economics—and playing cricket and hanging out with friends, like any other normal student. (Though she's met many important people through her humanitarian work— from President Obama to the Queen of England—Malala says her school friends have always helped to remind her "you're not that old yet, and you can have fun. You can be cheeky. You can love. You can smile. And I'm really grateful for that.")

But as often as she can, Malala continues to advocate for girls' education through the organization she started with her father, the Malala Fund. The work can be daunting at times. There are 130 million girls around the world who still do not have the benefit of education. And poverty is one of the biggest barriers to education. But she already sees good progress in Pakistan and other places, including parts of Africa, Asia, and Latin America, where they've empowered local leaders to push for more girls' education. And Malala's hopeful that more girls everywhere—once they experience and appreciate the benefits of schooling themselves—will be able to speak out and push for even more progress. "We are expanding our work and I can already see an impact," she said in 2018. "Because once you empower young girls, they can make change. I was a young girl, I raised my voice, and I could change the world. And I believe that there are other young girls out there—if we give them support, they can raise their voice and they can change the world."

"ONE CHILD, ONE TEACHER, ONE BOOK, AND ONE PEN CAN CHANGE THE WORLD."

Madison Stewart

MAKE YOUR CASE WITH **MOVIES**

By the time Madison Stewart was just 12 years old, she was scuba diving regularly with her father along the Gold Coast of Australia. One of her favorite places to dive was the Great Barrier Reef, where she swam alongside sharks. "The sharks, the Great Barrier Reef, and the oceans worldwide became my normality, my classroom, and my home," said Madison about her childhood. To Madison, the sharks were "like dogs or puppies playing in the water."

By 14, Madison was homeschooled on her family's boat. She began to notice something: each time she dove, she saw fewer and fewer sharks. This was alarming, because sharks are apex predators, which means they're at the top of the food chain, an important part of the ocean's ecosystem. Without sharks, the reefs can't thrive. What was going on? Madison asked around, and she learned that the Australian government had legalized shark fishing inside the Great Barrier Reef. The East Coast Inshore Fin Fish Fishery was now killing as many as 100,000 sharks there per year—legally.

Madison decided that if the government could see what she saw underwater, they wouldn't let the fishery continue. She bought an underwater video camera and made a film. She sent it to Australia's Minister for Environment Protection, Heritage and the Arts, along with a letter appealing to him not to renew the fishery's license for another four years. He didn't respond.

So Madison talked to law students and researchers and developed several documents supporting the cause of ending shark fishing. She collected 2,500 signatures to send to the Department of Fisheries. In return, she received a form letter, and that was it. "Sharks are being killed for food, fins, medicine, and fun," said Madison. "There is no end to the threats they face. But the biggest of all these is the human mentality towards them, because this stops people from fighting for them."

Shark fin soup is a delicacy in Chinese culture, and shark cartilage is often used—without measurable benefit—in medicine. Shark finning is an especially cruel and wasteful practice. Typically, after fishermen remove a shark's fin, they dump the shark back into the ocean. The shark is still alive but can't swim, so it is left to die or be eaten alive by other fish. There are also people who hunt sharks for sport.

Madison wants to change all of that, which starts with changing people's poor opinion of sharks. With her films, Madison shows people that sharks aren't killing machines, but are actually timid and prefer to be left alone. Also, sharks eat old, sick, and slow fish, which keeps the population healthier. Sharks help to keep many populations of sea life at the right size so that other prey species don't become too numerous. Scientists consider sharks a "keystone"

BEFRIEND YOUR FOE

Another of Madison's tactics is to identify people who are killing sharks in large numbers—and make friends with them. For example, a fisherman in Miami, Florida, known as "Mark the Shark" takes people out to kill sharks for fun. Madison reached out to Mark, and they became friends. Now, Mark still hunts sharks, but he releases more than he ever has, instead of killing every shark he catches. She's taken Mark's young children swimming with sharks, hoping they will not continue their father's practices once they grow up. When filming the ocean conservation documentary *Blue*, Madison also made friends with shark fishermen in Lombok, Indonesia. Since then, she's been working to influence the villagers there to focus more on tourism than on shark hunting, which could pull the village out of poverty while also protecting the fish.

species, which means that removing them causes the whole system to collapse, and that could mean the extinction of any number of other sea creatures.

"My films are the medium I use to spark awareness," said Madison. "I made them because I was desperate to raise a message through a mass of people who could help me." One of her many short films on YouTube, *Man Eating Shark*, got the attention of a film company. And, in 2014, she became the subject of a documentary called *Shark Girl*, which follows Madison while she swims with sharks and fights the fishing industry.

Madison has visited fisheries in many countries, but, she says, you don't have to travel the world to make change. To join the fight against shark hunting, Madison recommends starting simple and local. She's been all over the world to film shark fishing and raise public awareness, but, as she says, it all comes down to what's for sale on the shelves at the local store. Many restaurants in some states still sell shark meat, and you can ask to have it taken off the menu. You can also write to the government to support bans on fin fishing and to the media to disapprove of demonizing sharks in TV and films.

"I MAKE FILMS THAT CHANGE PEOPLE'S MINDS."

"You can start with simple things," she advises, like "educating the people around you, and being a shining example that change is not only possible but fun." Madison is actively spreading her message and sharing her films on social media, including Instagram and Facebook. "Write to me—reach out to me—I am here to help, I am taking it day by day as well, so let's figure this out together."

Alicia Garza, Patrisse Khan-Cullors, and Opal Tometi

ENCOURAGE LEADERSHIP TO BLOOM FROM THE **GROUND UP**

These days, the message "Black Lives Matter" pops up on T-shirts, bumper stickers, lawn signs, and in huge block letters spray-painted across highway overpasses. It's a common-sense reminder. It's a rallying cry for confronting the problem of racism and other types of misconduct toward African Americans, wherever they occur. And it's *also* the name of a major new civil rights movement.

But before it became all of those things, the phrase "black lives matter" originated when one of the movement's founders, Alicia Garza, was writing on Facebook. It was July 2013. Like many other people, she was rocked by the news that George Zimmerman, a Florida man who'd shot and killed an unarmed black 17-year-old named Trayvon Martin, was cleared of murder charges in his trial. At the time, Alicia worked for a San Francisco labor organization dedicated to protecting the employment and housing rights of working-class people of color. She wanted to reach out and offer her friends and fellow activists a message of hope in a dark time. "The sad part is," she wrote, "there's a section of America who is cheering and celebrating right now. and that makes me sick to my stomach. we GOTTA get it together y'all." Later, she added, "Btw stop saying we are not surprised. that's a damn shame in itself. I continue to be surprised at how little Black lives matter. And I will continue that.

stop giving up on black life." Wrapping up her post, she wrote, "Black people. I love you. I love us. Our lives matter."

Alicia's heartfelt message—she called it a "love letter to black people"—struck a chord with the people who read it. Patrisse Khan-Cullors, a fellow activist based in Los Angeles, read Alicia's post. She posted her own angry reaction to the verdict. She attached a new hashtag—#BlackLivesMatter—and shared Alicia's message on Twitter. The message continued to spread. And then another fellow activist friend of Alicia's got involved. Opal Tometi, a writer and immigration-rights organizer in New York, built public platforms for the slogan on Facebook, Tumblr, and Twitter. Activists and others inspired by the message could connect with one another on these platforms.

The Black Lives Matter (BLM) movement, which Alicia, Patrisse, and Opal officially founded in 2013, gathered even more steam the following summer. In August 2014, an 18-year-old named Michael Brown was shot and killed by a police officer in Ferguson, Missouri. Patrisse co-coordinated a freedom ride to protest Brown's killing. (The action was named in honor of the famous freedom rides of the 1960s, when integrated groups, known as freedom riders, traveled together on buses into the South to protest the segregation laws in place at the time.) The Black Life Matters Ride brought people

LOCAL VICTORIES

Each Black Lives Matter group in the network focuses on whatever actions their communities need most. A group of activists in Baton Rouge, Louisiana, for example, filed a lawsuit against police who beat them while they protested the killing of a black man. The city council offered them a $100,000 settlement. When BLM activists in Chicago learned that officers had withheld video footage of the killing of an unarmed teenager for over a year, they pressured the police for change. The superintendent of police was forced to resign. And in California, BLM activists helped pass two laws in 2018. One law allows public access to the records of police departments' own internal investigations of police shootings. The other requires police to release body camera footage within 45 days of an officer shooting. Both are key victories that will make it much more difficult for police to cover up unjust killings.

from all over the country together in Ferguson over Labor Day weekend of 2014. About 600 people, including some who'd never taken any political action before, participated in the protest. Once in Ferguson, they joined local protesters to rally against the uneven and unnecessarily violent way that police often target black people in our society. While they were in the greater St. Louis area (which Ferguson is part of), the new BLM activists met to discuss how they could push for change back in their own hometowns.

Today the organization has more than 40 local chapters. Alicia, Patrisse, and Opal purposefully never issued one-size-fits-all instructions for every BLM group to follow. Instead, they encouraged groups to operate without single leaders or hierarchies, so everyone in the groups can contribute on equal terms. They were fed up with older versions of civil rights activism in which, as they saw it, powerful straight black men often pushed women and others aside so they could hold on to the power and spotlight. Patrisse noted in a 2018 interview that "we've laid a foundation around challenging patriarchy," the automatic assumption that men should always hold the most power. And, as Alicia noted in a 2016 interview, the BLM movement represents a shift in civil rights activism because it intentionally welcomes all people—regardless of race, gender, sexual identity, or class—to contribute. "If we demonstrate a collective commitment and a collective practice" while fighting for change, she said, "then we have a real shot for living in a world that is more just, more equitable—in a world where black lives actually do matter."

> **"WE'RE PART OF A MOVEMENT THAT'S BEEN HAPPENING FOR HUNDREDS OF YEARS, AND THIS JUST HAPPENS TO BE A TIPPING POINT."**
>
> —PATRISSE KHAN-CULLORS

Amythest Schaber

SPREAD SOME **UNDERSTANDING**

As a child in British Columbia, Canada, Amythest Schaber felt different from other kids. Reading and writing came early, but socializing was tricky. Amythest, who uses the pronouns *they, them*, and *theirs*, was clumsy and had a tendency to rapidly move their arms. This made them stand out so much that other children would be mocked just for playing with them.

So they tried to hide their differences—the things that made Amythest Amythest. But by the time they were in college, Amythest was dealing with so much anxiety and depression that they left school in 2012. A mental health professional suggested they might have autism, which Amythest describes as "a pervasive, neurological, developmental condition that affects about 1% of human beings." They explain that autism affects every part of a person: personality, experiences, memories, and how they grow up, communicate, think, and move. Still, it was not until Amythest was 22 that they were assessed by a psychologist and an occupational therapist. After several appointments and many questions, they said, "'Yup, you sure are autistic,'" as Amythest later recalled.

Amythest points out that autism is not an illness or disease, but a naturally occurring variation in the human brain. There have always been autistic people but, for a long time, society simply didn't recognize them as autistic.

The clumsiness that caused Amythest such trouble in school was actually motor dyspraxia, a disorder that makes it difficult to perform certain kinds of tasks. And the arm movements? That's a kind of self-stimulation, often called stimming, that is common to autistic people.

Amythest had long suspected they were autistic, and now they had confirmation. It was a relief. In fact, Amythest soon discovered a world full of other people very much like them. "Things only clicked for me when I found the words of actual autistic people in the form of blog posts and essays," Amythest says. "It was listening to other autistic people talk about their experiences that was the most helpful for me and led to me realizing that, yes, I am autistic. I want my work to be that for other people. I want to be a source of information for people who are wondering if they are autistic or who want to learn more about what being autistic means."

People who are allistic, or not autistic, can learn from Amythest too. On their Tumblr, Neurowonderful, Amythest writes about disability, autism, and neurodiversity (the wide range of differences in brain function and behavior, including autism disorders). They also launched a YouTube series called "Ask an Autistic" to explain the positive and difficult aspects of being autistic in a world that can be dismissive and downright hostile to people with disabilities. For the viewer who only has time to watch one video, they recommend the 10th one, "How to Be an Ally."

DON'T LET DOUBT SLOW YOU DOWN

While fighting for a cause, no one is going to be 100% perfect all the time. Amythest admitted that they don't always feel confident. They regret that low self-esteem can prevent them from going after opportunities. "Many people struggle with feeling like they are not good enough. Even the most respected writers, artists, athletes, scientists, or activists can have times when they feel like an impostor, and girls and women know this especially well." To deal with impostor syndrome, Amythest has a suggestion: "The important thing is to recognize that these feelings are not worth listening to and to not let them stop you from pursuing what is important to you."

Amythest wanted their voice to counter harmful messages "and spread some understanding." (They have even created bold, stylish T-shirts with slogans like "All Kinds of Bodies, All Kinds of Brains.") Sometimes the topics they discuss are serious, such as when Amythest speaks out for disabled people who are hurt or abused by people who believe they make no contribution to the world around them. And sometimes the topics are lighter, but equally illuminating. The stimming that Amythest was made to feel ashamed of? "Stimmy joy is something that I don't think non-autistic people experience," they explain, "and it's one of the most beautiful parts of being autistic." The fact that there is beauty and diversity in autism is still unknown to too many people. Amythest believes that efforts to eradicate autism "have damaged the diversity, the beautiful, complex, colorful diversity of humanity."

Amythest is now reaching more people than ever. Their YouTube channel has more than 45,000 subscribers, and their videos have been translated into a dozen languages, including Japanese, Swedish, German, and Hebrew. Universities and professional training programs use Amythest's work in psychology courses and professional programs. Autism has helped, not hurt, Amythest's activism. "Something special about being autistic," they say, "is how passionate I am about what I care about. Sometimes it feels like the force of my caring could power a small city."

> **"WHEN I STARTED OUT IN MY ACTIVISM, I DIDN'T THINK MY VIDEOS WOULD GET MANY VIEWS AT ALL. I JUST WANTED TO COUNTERACT THE HARMFUL MESSAGES ABOUT AUTISM AND SPREAD SOME UNDERSTANDING."**

Maysoon Zayid

MAKE YOUR ENEMY **LAUGH**

Stand-up comic Maysoon Zayid knows the difference between being laughed at and making people laugh. Maysoon has cerebral palsy. She can stand only for brief periods, so she calls herself a "sit-down stand-up comedian." And rather than hiding the disability that makes her tremble constantly, she sometimes makes it her opening joke. "I'm not drunk," she says, "but the doctor who delivered me was."

Cerebral palsy is not the only part of Maysoon's identity that makes her stand out from the overwhelmingly white, male, and nondisabled landscape of television and comedy. She often uses the things that make her different as one of her other opening jokes. "I'm Palestinian, Muslim, I'm a woman of color, I'm disabled," Maysoon explains. Then she adds sadly, "And I live in New Jersey."

When she was growing up, Maysoon's family and friends never belittled or talked down to her, so it was a shock when, for example, a college professor asked if she could read. She originally wanted to be a dramatic actor but realized people who looked like her "didn't exist really on TV."

"People with disabilities are the largest minority in the world," Maysoon points out in her 2013 TED Talk, "and we are the most underrepresented in entertainment." Maysoon has worked hard to change that. She cofounded and coproduces the New York Arab-

American Comedy Festival and has appeared on Comedy Central's online series *The Watch List*. She is one of five comedians featured in *STAND UP: Muslim American Comics Come of Age*, part of PBS's *America at a Crossroads* documentary series. And her TED Talk was translated into more than 40 languages and is one of the most watched talks in the program's history.

In 2018, ABC ordered a pilot for Maysoon's sitcom, *Can-Can*. (That means the network liked her idea so much that they agreed to pay to make the first episode of a potential TV series). In *Can-Can*, she stars as a Muslim restaurant critic with cerebral palsy. Maysoon wants the show to demonstrate the diversity within Islam, noting, "I am not used to seeing characters on TV who are Muslim who don't have accents."

Maysoon does not limit her activism to the entertainment world. She started a nonprofit organization called Maysoon's Kids. From 2003 to 2012, Maysoon's Kids helped run welfare programs and training sessions for parents and teachers of disabled Palestinian children, supplying them with "sign-language interpreters, voice-activated computers, social workers, teachers. . . . We did everything we could do to help."

Despite the work she was already doing, for a long time Maysoon didn't consider herself a disability advocate. But as her profile rose, she experienced so much mockery online that "I realized that the disability was a much, much, much, bigger thing than I had ever admitted. I realize that I have no choice but to go on because I have to go on for the disabled kids who can't."

There's still a lot of work to do to ensure equality for those kids. For instance, Maysoon wants to make sure that kids with disabilities have access to education. She also hopes "to see the end of the offensive practice of nondisabled actors playing visibly disabled on screen," she says. "I hope by bringing laughter to the world, I can get people to realize that being a bigot and a bully is bad, while being an equality junkie is a party. I hope future generations will shun supremacy and embrace democracy. I also hope they find a way to translate what cats are saying when they meow."

Maysoon has long been a passionate political advocate—she was a delegate at the 2008 Democratic National Convention and has worked with several New Jersey governors. She has become an advocate for Muslims and Arabs in the United States too. After 9/11, she wanted to counteract the stereotype of the dangerous Arab terrorist. Sadly, in 2015, after the rise of Donald Trump, she became the target of a surge of death threats and cyberstalking.

But Maysoon believes comedy can do more than entertain. "If you can get your enemy to laugh, they are less likely to hunt you, to hate you. I have changed people's minds. You can't change everybody, but I have changed a lot of people." She also reminds budding activists that it's okay to have other interests, to take breaks and do something fun like yoga, dancing, or "binge-watching hours of *Bob's Burgers*."

Pound the pavement, if you can, she says. But "don't let anyone tell you that sharing on the Internet is not activism," she says. "We do what our bodies allow us to, and every bit counts."

"MY ADVICE FOR BUDDING ACTIVISTS—IT IS OKAY TO HAVE FUN."

Eleanor Roosevelt

SPEAK UP FOR HUMAN RIGHTS (AND STEP AWAY FROM ORGANIZATIONS THAT DON'T)

Before her husband, Franklin, became president, Eleanor Roosevelt, the longest-serving First Lady in US history, worked passionately to help people who were struggling to get by. While Franklin rose up the ranks in politics, Eleanor raised their five children. On top of that, she showed up regularly to serve meals at soup kitchens and mop floors at military hospitals. Collaborating with a few friends, she even started a furniture company in upstate New York to help local farmers who were barely scraping by.

Franklin became president in 1933. But Eleanor knew she didn't want to just stay home in the White House serving tea to the wives of visiting dignitaries, so she found new ways to help others.

Eleanor had gotten some great advice from a woman named Lorena Hickok, a newspaper writer she'd befriended during the presidential campaign, and she decided to give it a go. Two days after Franklin's inauguration in 1933, Eleanor gathered 35 female journalists and announced she'd be holding regular press conferences open only to female reporters. This not only forced newspapers to hire more women writers but also gave Eleanor many opportunities over the years to speak out about issues she cared about, including women's rights, immigrants' rights, and the new job and housing programs designed to help people get back on their feet that her husband was developing. (These programs were part of the New Deal, the president's economic-recovery program.)

Eleanor realized how powerfully her own actions could influence public opinion. She traveled across the country—often in a car she drove herself, against the advice of Secret Service agents—to find out what hardships people were facing and how she and Franklin could improve their lives. But one unexpected event back in Washington shined a memorable spotlight on racial discrimination in the United States.

> **"IF SILENCE SEEMS TO GIVE APPROVAL, THEN REMAINING SILENT IS COWARDLY."**

Eleanor was a member of the Daughters of the American Revolution (DAR), an elite group of women who traced their family trees back to the American Revolution. In 1939, the DAR barred opera singer Marian Anderson from performing in its auditorium in Constitution Hall because Anderson was black. In response, Eleanor resigned from the group. In her resignation letter, Eleanor said that the DAR had "an opportunity to lead in an enlightened way" but had "failed to do so."

She also wrote about her decision to quit in her own widely read newspaper column, "My Day." Then she helped the National Association for the Advancement of Colored People (NAACP), the secretary of the interior, and others arrange for Anderson to sing at the Lincoln Memorial instead. This landmark concert drew more than 70,000 people to Washington on Easter Sunday. People came to hear Anderson's magnificent voice, but also because they'd seen the First Lady take a bold stand against racism and wanted to show their support too. Eleanor understood that getting good media coverage could amplify powerful messages. So she not only pressured radio stations to broadcast the concert but encouraged the NAACP to use recordings of Anderson's concert in their fundraising campaigns.

Eleanor went on to help people and fight for justice in other important ways. During World War II, she traveled to US military hospitals and to US bases abroad to visit troops, thanking them for their service and sacrifice. Seeing the rise of anti-Jewish sentiment in Germany also made her more disgusted with racial segregation in America. Why were people rightly willing to fight Hitler but so unwilling to confront the prejudice occurring every day on military bases, in schools, and in cities all across the United States?

Writing in the *New Republic* in 1942, she asked her fellow citizens to consider the true cost of denying the bigotry and discrimination that was rampant here. "One of the main destroyers of freedom is our attitude toward the colored race," she wrote. And with sharp words like these—plus showing the nation and the world that she would rather quit a racist group than stifle her beliefs—Eleanor became an important early white supporter of the African-American civil rights movement.

For Eleanor, living according to her values was always worth the cost. "Courage is more exhilarating than fear," Eleanor wrote in her memoir *You Learn by Living*, "and in the long run it is easier."

HUMAN RIGHTS FOR ALL

After Franklin died in 1945, Eleanor became a US delegate to the United Nations, the new organization dedicated to promoting world peace that she helped Franklin envision before he died. As the elected chair of a new UN committee known as the Human Rights Commission, she negotiated tirelessly with a group of mostly male international diplomats. Together they hammered out an agreement known as the Universal Declaration of Human Rights. The document, finalized in December 1948, clearly spelled out the rights to safety, equality, and justice that all people in the world were entitled to. After the UN General Assembly formally accepted the declaration, the entire assembly of delegates rose up to give Eleanor a standing ovation. Eleanor considered it her most important achievement. The principles laid out in the document still stand at the center of many countries' constitutions and guide international laws.

Lilly Ledbetter

FIGHT **TODAY** FOR A BETTER TOMORROW

It was a very quiet form of protest that inspired Lilly Ledbetter to become an activist: In 1998, she received an anonymous, handwritten note. "When I found the note, life as I knew it ended," wrote Lilly in her autobiography, *Grace and Grit: My Fight for Equal Pay and Fairness at Goodyear and Beyond.* The note was left for Lilly at her workplace. She was an area manager for the Goodyear Tire and Rubber Company in Gasden, Alabama.

One of the rules at Goodyear was that employees weren't allowed to discuss their salaries—they would be fired if they did. So Lilly was surprised to find that the note listed the salaries of three other area managers, all of whom were men. And each of these men was earning a lot more money than Lilly. "We had the exact same job," said Lilly in an interview. "It was so devastating. It didn't just impact my pay, it impacted my overtime, my family, and my future."

Lilly went home and talked to her husband. Even though she was just two years away from retiring and they knew it would be a long and stressful struggle, they decided to file a discrimination lawsuit. A year later, a jury in the Alabama District Court agreed that Lilly had been wronged and ordered Goodyear to pay her $300,000. But Goodyear appealed the decision, and the case went all the way to the Supreme Court.

> **"I'VE REALIZED THAT THE TRUE TEST OF AN INDIVIDUAL IS NOT SO MUCH WHAT HAPPENS TO HER, BUT HOW SHE REACTS TO IT. WHEN WE SEE AN INJUSTICE, DO WE SIT AND DO NOTHING, OR DO WE FIGHT BACK?"**

Lilly lost. In a 5-4 decision in 2007, the Supreme Court ruled that she wasn't entitled to compensation because she hadn't complained within 180 days of her first unequal paycheck, which was what the law required. This is what's known as a technicality, or a small detail in a rule or law. How could she have complained within 180 days if she didn't even know about it until two decades later?

The Supreme Court followed the letter of the law, though the law itself was clearly flawed. People took notice—including President Obama, who signed the Lilly Ledbetter Fair Pay Act in 2009. This new law allows workers to sue when they learn they've been cheated, regardless of when they got their first paycheck.

Today, women still earn just 80 cents for every dollar made by men (and women of color earn even less). "Those pennies add up to real money," said Lilly. "It's real money for the little things, like being able to take your kids to the movies, and for the big things, like sending them to college." Equal pay isn't a reality yet, but it will be. And many people's lives have changed for the better because of the law that bears Lilly's name.

Lilly never did receive compensation for the pay she lost, but she has her eye on the big picture. "I'm hopeful that the Ledbetter Act will impact future generations, generations of women and men I will not live to see but my granddaughter and great-granddaughter will," she wrote in her book.

KEEP CALM

Learning to control your emotions is one of the most important lessons Lilly has learned—and hopes to impart to future activists. "I learned never to let anything make me mad, because anger causes a person to lose focus and energy needed to achieve goals," she said in an interview. "Everyone can be more successful in life if they don't let anger affect them. Set goals, plan, and work to achieve them."

Rosa Parks

TAKE A **BOLD STAND** (OR A SEAT!) AGAINST STUPID RULES

"**N**ah. —Rosa Parks, 1955." That's the message written across a cool T-shirt commemorating a defining moment in the civil rights movement. With a remarkable act of calm refusal, Rosa Parks, a 42-year-old seamstress in Montgomery, Alabama, inspired many other people to defy local discriminatory laws and traditions that treated African Americans as second-class citizens.

Rosa was riding a city bus home from work on December 1, 1955. At the time, segregation rules stated that black people had to sit in the middle and back of the public buses and give up their seats if white people needed more room (the first four rows of seats were already reserved for whites). She wasn't planning to protest the rules that evening. An active member of Montgomery's local chapter of the National Association for the Advancement of Colored People (NAACP), Rosa still had more work to do that night. When she got home, she had to send out notices about the NAACP's upcoming election of officers.

But then a group of white people boarded the bus. One man was left standing. All the seats at the front of the bus were filled by white passengers, so the driver ordered four

black people sitting in the middle seats, including Rosa, to get up and surrender their seats so this new white passenger could have the entire middle section of the bus all to himself. And Rosa, fed up by this and so many other nonsensical rules that gave white people special privileges, just said "no." Speaking of her refusal to follow the bus driver's order in a television documentary she said, "When he saw me still sitting . . . he asked if I was going to stand up. I told him, 'No, I'm not.' And he said, 'Well, if you don't stand up, I'm going to have to call the policeman and have you arrested.' I said, 'You may do that.'"

Rosa was jailed overnight. Word of her dignified civil disobedience quickly spread. Less than a week after Rosa's arrest, most black commuters in Montgomery began a boycott of the buses that lasted 381 days. Some boycotters had to walk as far as 20 miles a day. On November 13, 1956, the Supreme Court declared Montgomery's segregation laws unconstitutional. Montgomery authorities received a court order forcing them to drop their discriminatory seating policy on December 20. And the next day, when the boycott ended, Rosa took her own seat on her regular bus, sitting right up near the front.

Thanks to Rosa Parks (who many call the "mother of the civil rights movement"), civil rights advocates learned a valuable lesson about the power of individual action: sometimes it only takes one courageous person, making a bold stand, to kick-start a big change.

"I WAS WILLING TO GET ARRESTED— IT WAS **WORTH** THE CONSEQUENCES."

LaDonna Redmond

ENGAGE YOUR COMMUNITY

When LaDonna Redmond was pregnant with her first child, Wade, she used to lie awake at night and wonder how she could keep her baby safe. The question became even more urgent after the baby was born, because Wade had serious allergies to dairy, eggs, peanuts, and shellfish (like shrimp, crabs, and lobster). Eating any of these foods could be deadly. More than once, LaDonna and her husband raced to the emergency room when Wade struggled to breathe during an allergic reaction. One day, as LaDonna gazed at her child, connected to a breathing machine, she swore that her family would never come back to the hospital that way again.

Because of Wade's allergies, LaDonna could not feed them packaged, processed food—those foods tended to contain the dangerous allergens. (Wade, who died at age 20 in 2018, used the pronouns *they*, *them*, and *theirs*.) But it was incredibly difficult to feed her family *without* those products. "In my neighborhood," LaDonna once said, "I can buy designer gym shoes, every kind of fast food, every kind of junk food, all kinds of malt liquor and illegal drugs, and maybe even a semiautomatic weapon, but I cannot purchase an organic tomato."

She would drive all over Chicago to get organic food, which she sometimes found at co-op grocery stores, a kind of store she hadn't known existed. (A cooperative grocery store, or *co-op*, is a store that sells to everyone but offers lower prices to the members of the cooperative and focuses on community enrichment, education, and development. Members can also vote on the choices and direction of a co-op.) LaDonna finally found the food she was looking for at co-ops, but there were none in her neighborhood.

"All I wanted was fresh food," she said, "produce without harmful pesticides and meat without antibiotics. But living on the West Side of Chicago meant I had to leave my community, and shopping trips were expensive, not only in terms of the cost of the food I bought, but the gas I used and time I spent." She could see that the limited access to healthy food affected others too. A steady diet of the highly processed, prepackaged food available in LaDonna's neighborhood also has long-term effects like obesity, diabetes, and heart disease.

LaDonna already had a long history of working to uplift her community. She had founded a recovery home called Sister House and had worked to ensure reproductive rights, safe housing, and support for women returning from prison or drug treatment. And she had learned from her teachers and mentors that women are powerful and that there is great strength in "showing up strong, showing up well, looking my best, doing my best, on behalf of [my] community."

Now she discovered that her activism had prepared her well to be a parent. "My journey with my first child," she has said, "would require all the skills and more that I learned in my life as a community organizer." She began by trying to bring fresh vegetables to neighborhoods that needed them. She and her husband formed a nonprofit and obtained several vacant lots. "We converted those lots to urban farm sites," LaDonna explains, "and we hired people from the community to work on those sites." She also launched a victorious campaign to get salad bars where Chicago Public Schools had once sold junk food.

When communities lack food, she has said, it's evidence of injustice that has its roots in capitalism and racism. "Food justice means we talk about the things that help people get food. For example, raising the minimum wage would help people have food. Making sure our immigration policies are fair to those harvesting our food; making sure that women with children have childcare so that they can work— 'food justice' links all of these different issues."

LaDonna cofounded a group that paired universities with their surrounding neighborhoods to address food access and public health in African-American communities. Later, she moved to Minneapolis and, in 2013, she launched the Campaign for Food Justice Now, which identifies and addresses issues of social justice, gender, class, and race in the food system. She also took a job with a cooperative grocery. "I can name about 50 projects right now, areas where we need to grow," she said. "The work is always the work. It's never going to be, 'Oh, we've arrived, and we are done.'"

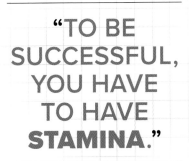

WORK WITH YOUR NEIGHBORS

In Minneapolis, the Seward Community Co-op wanted to open a second location in the Bryant neighborhood, whose residents are predominately people of color. But the community was leery of the co-op's potential effects on the neighborhood. "Communities of color require a conversation," LaDonna said. "You can't just mail them a flyer and think they're going to go, 'Oh, this is wonderful.' You have to get out and meet people." It's important to anticipate and answer people's questions. Would the new store lead to higher rent? Would it sell food no one there could afford? Would the new jobs go to anyone who already lived in Bryant? LaDonna, who had once been the sole person of color at Chicago food co-ops and food activism meetings, joined the co-op as community education coordinator. With a lot of cooperation, conversation, and work, the new co-op has become a success in its neighborhood. LaDonna is proud that it is "inspiring a generation of food co-ops that take diversity, equity, and inclusion very seriously."

Jennifer Flynn Walker

ASK **TOUGH** QUESTIONS (THEN RECORD WHAT HAPPENS)

In 2016, activist Jennifer Flynn Walker was considering stepping away from mobilizing. "I felt like I had contributed what I had to contribute," she says. Then Donald Trump was elected president—and Jennifer returned to the front lines.

She's still fighting the powerful when their policies harm the weak, but it is true that Jennifer, who works for the Center for Popular Democracy, has contributed a lot already. One of her early campaigns as an activist was to help homeless people with AIDS find safe housing in New York City. Along with other activists, she helped people navigate a system that was forcing them to seek shelter on subways or in parks. They also made sure the media kept covering the crisis.

The fight to house people with AIDS showed that sometimes a person can accomplish the most by showing up and asking officials for help face-to-face. This technique was widely used after Trump's election, when Republicans tried harder than ever to repeal the Affordable Care Act (ACA), or Obamacare. Getting rid of the ACA could have led to fewer protections for people with certain medical conditions or to cuts in funding that would hurt people who rely on government programs to stay alive and functional. So, in the spring of 2017, Jennifer and many others joined forces to confront elected

> ## "I NEVER FEEL AS FREE AND POWERFUL AS WHEN I'M WORKING WITH OTHERS TO ENGAGE IN **POWERFUL DIRECT ACTION**."

officials in person—at their offices, at fundraisers, at town hall meetings—to ask them whether they would vote to protect the ACA. The tactic of confrontation is called birddogging. It is a targeted plan to ask direct questions of politicians.

"Birddogging is one of my favorite tools, because it's one of the few where you get to talk directly to the person who makes the decision," says Jennifer. Sometimes this interaction helps persuade a politician to change his or her vote.

Her fellow organizer Paul Davis had used birddogging effectively under previous administrations. So after Trump's election, Paul, his colleague Jaron Benjamin, and Jennifer began setting up trainings. The activists, who call themselves Birddog Nation, do not have an official leader. Members of the group go around the country and try to get politicians to answer direct questions and state their positions clearly and on the record (especially when the politicians try to avoid it!). They also try to sway politicians to vote against harmful policies.

Birddogging isn't as simple as it sounds. Organizers have to find out where a politician will be and get past their handlers, who will

often try to prevent questioning. Activists have learned to keep their queries firm, pointed, and direct. They practice questions ahead of time to help calm their nerves. They spread out at political events, raise their hands "first, fast, and high" at question time (and sometimes even when there is no designated question time). They also make sure someone else records the interaction so that there is a record of the conversation to share on social media. Some officials would prefer to control their words in a prepared statement, but pointed, persistent questioning can reveal the actual effects of a law or policy.

Jennifer and Birddog Nation won the fight to protect the ACA, but they don't win every time. Protesters flooded Washington, DC, to fight sweeping tax cuts in 2017, which later passed. They also fought unsuccessfully to keep Brett Kavanaugh, who was accused of assaulting Christine Blasey Ford as a teenager, from being appointed to the Supreme Court in 2018.

But Jennifer isn't backing down. She tries to remind citizens that they do not need to wait to start making a difference. "I hope that others recognize that they have everything they need to change the world right now," she says. "They don't have to learn every single thing about an issue. They don't have to be a better speaker. They don't have to wait for someone else to join them. You are the one everyone else is waiting for."

Birddog Nation is still expanding. Over the past few years, Jennifer and her colleagues have trained at least 6,000 people in 125 cities and 40 states, giving them the tools and encouragement to ask vital questions of people in power—people who have the responsibility to answer them.

LEARN THE ART OF BIRDDOGGING

Activists like Jennifer encourage people—whether they've worked on many campaigns or are first-timers—to get involved. Policies about health care, education, housing, clean drinking water, and more are decided by people who participate in the political process. Jennifer recommends checking out the Town Hall Project (townhallproject.com) to find information on having face-to-face conversations with federal elected officials. She also encourages people interested in being trained in birddogging to get in touch with her (jflynn@populardemocracy.org) or to contact Paul Davis or Jaron Benjamin, who work on national advocacy for Housing Works. If you can gather 15 people together in a space, they'll come to you.

Shirin Ebadi

PUSH FOR LEGAL CHANGE

To say that the Iranian lawyer, judge, and Nobel Peace Prize-winning human rights activist Shirin Ebadi has bravely weathered many ups and downs is putting it mildly.

Born in 1947, Shirin had the good fortune to be raised in a loving family that believed women are capable of doing anything. She received a great education (her father was a law professor and author). And, in 1969, she became one of the country's first female judges. She went on to earn a doctorate degree in law, graduating with honors in 1971. And in 1975, she became the first woman ever to serve as president of the city court of Tehran, Iran's capital city.

Shirin's high-profile work as a judge gave her and others new hope that Iran was finally moving closer toward upholding the commitment it made in its 1906 constitution granting all citizens equal rights. But soon their hope was sorely challenged.

In 1979, Islamic fundamentalists seized control of Iran's government. Shirin, a devout Muslim, originally supported this revolution. The country's new leaders believed women should be subservient to men, so they demoted Shirin and other female judges, making them low-level administrative clerks in the same courts they'd formerly presided over. "It took scarcely a month for me to realize that, in fact, I had willingly and enthusiastically participated in my own demise," Shirin wrote in her autobiography *Iran Awakening*.

"I was a woman, and this revolution's victory demanded my defeat."

She left the court system in frustration but, after years of lobbying, was finally able to earn a license to practice law in 1992. Working as a lawyer, she took on many high-profile cases, fearlessly defending the rights of women, children, journalists, and other people facing discrimination and abuse for their religious beliefs.

Though many admired Shirin for taking on challenging cases, others saw her work advocating for women's rights as disrespecting Islamic law. But her determination to help Iranian women overcome oppression was steadfast. The Iranian government claims that laws restricting women's rights are in line with the Islamic religion, but Shirin is determined to prove that "with a correct interpretation of Islam, we can have equal rights for women," as she has said. Like any religion, "there is not a single interpretation of Islam."

Shirin faced regular rebukes from judges and, occasionally, death threats. Once, while she was reviewing official documents in preparation for a trial, Shirin was startled to find her own name on a list of people that government ministers had targeted for assassination because they'd dared to criticize the government.

But Shirin was more pleasantly surprised when she learned that she'd been awarded the Nobel Peace Prize in 2003. She was the first Iranian woman and the first Muslim woman to receive the award, which is given annually to people who work hard to resolve disputes peacefully and democratically. Receiving the award helped to bring attention and international support to her humanitarian work. "Winning the Nobel Peace Prize meant that the world started to pay attention to the human rights activities of Muslim women," she once said. "After I won the prize, many discriminatory laws were changed." For example, in 2004, a law was changed to grant divorced Iranian women child custody rights for the first time.

However, Iranian officials were displeased that Shirin had become an international human rights star. They continued to punish her for her activism. She was threatened, detained, and interrogated. She set up an office in Tehran with some of the money from her Nobel Prize. She planned to house her human rights organization there, but it was raided and shut down by police. After her husband was arrested and seriously beaten in 2009, Shirin decided to leave Iran for her own safety. She now lives in London in exile. But she still speaks out courageously and persuasively against social, political, and economic injustice in Iran, Europe, the United States, or wherever she sees corruption operating in the world. "We have to put the spotlight on words that are abused, and we must illuminate dark spots where dictators are hiding," Shirin said in a 2017 speech hosted by the Nobel organization. "This is the duty of each and every one of us who believes in the future of humanity."

> **"I FIND PEACE OF MIND WHEN I RECOGNIZE THE DIFFERENCE BETWEEN WHAT CAN BE CHANGED AND WHAT CANNOT, AND THEN I FOCUS ALL MY ABILITIES ON WHAT I CAN CHANGE."**

Gloria Steinem

FIND YOUR FAMILY OF
FELLOW **ACTIVISTS**

During the 1960s and 1970s, many more women were beginning to understand how their lives were confined by certain societal roles. They were seen as wife, mother, secretary, or fill-in-the-blank female whose duties and opportunities were considered (for no good reason other than tradition) less important than men's. So when a charismatic political reporter named Gloria Steinem led a group of woman journalists and activists to launch a magazine dedicated to helping women choose new roles for themselves, it was an instant hit.

Gloria and her colleagues called the magazine *Ms.*, cleverly borrowing the title that (unlike Mrs. or Miss) refers to a woman without indicating her marital status. They ran articles on how to respond to discrimination in the workplace, how to divide household chores evenly in a marriage, and other useful topics covered almost nowhere else at the time. Their first issue, published in 1971, sold out in eight days.

But Gloria knew that women weren't only eager to read about how they could improve their personal and professional lives—they were also hungry to meet face-to-face. That way they could learn about new local initiatives to support women's rights and strategize about how to encourage politicians and companies to create better policies. They could also gain strength from seeing how many other women in the "sisterhood" (as Gloria called members of the growing women's movement) shared their concerns. So Gloria stepped up her already busy travel schedule. She visited college campuses and community centers in order to speak, organize gatherings, and spread the message of feminism, which she defines as simply recognizing the "equality and full humanity of women and men."

Gloria has been inspired by different ideas for fostering political action that she picked up on her own travels. In her early twenties, Gloria lived in India, writing guides for tourists. During her time there, she studied the nonviolent protest tactics of Mahatma Gandhi, the leader of the Indian independence movement against British rule. She also saw Indian villagers beset by riots relying on "talking circles"—community gatherings built on the Gandhian principle of speaking and listening equally with respect—to rebuild trust. And both experiences taught her to appreciate the "infinite amount of learning" that occurs when people sit down, look at each other eye to eye, and focus on finding peaceful solutions together.

In almost every major social movement, from the "women's movement to the civil rights movement to the Chinese revolution . . . all big change starts with small groups," she explained. "You can't do it by yourself. People are communal creatures. You need to have an alternate, regular place that's almost an alternate family where you can create a different set of possibilities, discover that you're not crazy—the *system* is crazy. And this needs to be a regular part of your life."

"REVOLUTIONS, LIKE HOUSES, GET BUILT FROM THE **BOTTOM UP**, NOT THE TOP DOWN."

Many things have changed since Gloria became the most famous leader of the feminist movement in the 1970s. But her faith that women (and men who care about women's rights) can accomplish great things when they sit down and put their heads together is as solid as ever. And she knows that they can find joy, support, and friendship along the way too. "Life is an organizing problem," she has said, explaining that she loves being an organizer. "Because you look at something and you think, 'That's not fair, but if we did this or that, maybe that would happen.' It's just infinitely interesting. It's so much fun. Don't accept things the way they are. It's so boring," she said. "Being an organizer . . . is like being a social entrepreneur. . . . And the reward for yourself is huge. You've made a difference. And not only that, but somebody in your office or in your family or on the street will come up to you and say, 'Thank you. You inspired me. I did this. You supported me.' What's better than that?"

TAKE YOUR MESSAGE ON THE ROAD

Now in her eighties, Gloria is still constantly on the move. She estimates that she's spent more than half her time over the past four decades traveling across the United States and around the world, working as a "wandering organizer," as she calls herself. On these trips, she learns about women's lives and raises awareness about key issues impacting women. Lately, she's especially interested in protecting women's reproductive rights and improving their economic status. Her radical in-person approach to advocacy is partly rooted in her upbringing. She grew up traveling with her beloved father, an antiques dealer who moved her family frequently. "I come by my road habits honestly," Gloria wrote in her 2015 autobiography, *My Life on the Road.*

Yara Shahidi

TAKE IT **STEP-BY-STEP**

Even as a child, Yara Shahidi had a lot of career plans. "I wanted to be a historian," she told journalist Elaine Welteroth, "and then I wanted to be a thought leader," someone whose ideas and opinions are widely respected. And she wanted to "help influence our political system, and amidst that, I wanted to be a professional Jet Ski rider and also work for the FBI." Even as she was planning all of that, she was also an actor who'd been making commercials since the age of two. By 2014, she was costarring in the hit ABC sitcom *Black-ish* and, in 2018, she began anchoring her own spinoff, *Grown-ish*. But just as when she was little, she has more than one goal. Yara doesn't allow her TV career to be an obstacle to creating social change. Instead she uses her fame to further her activism.

Yara embraces the fact that she is many things, and all of them are important. She is African American on her mother's side and Iranian American on her father's. She is both a young person—born in 2000 in Minnesota—and a leader. And she is a passionate political activist as well as an artist. "It is through my art," she explains, "that I have purposefully chosen to express my activism."

Yara does this by reaching out to young people through social media campaigns to urge them to take meaningful social and political action. She worked with the Young Women's Leadership Network to create Yara's Club, which gathers high school students for discussion and activism. In 2018, she launched Eighteen x 18, a campaign to educate young voters—many eligible to vote for the first time in that year's midterm elections—about issues like climate change, gun control, and reproductive rights.

Yara also joined the campaign Little by Little, which aims to unite young people in doing two billion acts of good by 2030. To explain Little by Little's approach, Yara has said, "The world has lots of problems, and they're big. So we need lots of solutions, and those can be small. . . . Finding solutions will happen quicker when we look for them together."

Yara admits that she doesn't always feel as confident as she seems. "As a teenager I'm very unsure of myself most of the time, not certain if I'm saying the right things, if I'm acting the right way, if I'm even supposed to be here," she has said. Sometimes she has to remind herself that she, too, has something to contribute. During a visit to the White House, Yara was discussing her desire to be a thought leader, when the woman she was speaking with "just kinda chuckled and said, 'You need credentials for that.'" Yara found the response disappointing. She grew up in a family that supported and encouraged her. "I come from the land of 'of course,'" she explains. "Like, 'of course this is going to happen' because we have willed it to be, and we are going to put in the work to make it happen."

The land of "of course" is a family with a long tradition of being activists and breaking new ground. Yara's grandfather was a member of the Black Panthers, a political organization formed in the 1960s to fight police brutality toward African Americans. Her cousin is an astronaut who went into space as the first female Iranian space tourist, and her aunt visited Rwanda to study how war-torn areas can heal after deep conflict. "I've been learning more and more about what the women in my family have accomplished, and it's extraordinary. Their dedication to people, to science, to community, to politics," Yara marvels. "But my mama, she's my first role model. She's really shown me how to be a woman of color." Yara's mother taught her that her opinion is worthy. "She taught me to understand that I am qualified for any of the conversations that I'm a part of, whether it's with executives or a school principal. I'm supposed to be there."

Yara is still many things: a college student at Harvard, a self-described "square" whose character on TV breaks many more rules than Yara does in real life, a fashionista, and a committed activist. She believes her generation will solve whatever issues it is confronted with. "And not with grand gestures," she adds, "but by the power of the compound effect, by doing little things over and over again. If we don't quit, we'll fix the world step-by-step."

"IT IS SO IMPORTANT TO MAKE IT OUR MISSION, ESPECIALLY IF YOU HAVE THE PRIVILEGE TO DO SO, TO **BE SOCIALLY AWARE** AND TO HELP OUR GLOBAL COMMUNITY."

Susan B. Anthony

DON'T LET SETBACKS DERAIL YOUR **PROGRESS**

The pioneering suffragist Susan B. Anthony was teaching school in the 1840s when her budding feminist instincts—and indignation—boiled over. Susan saw how unfairly she and other female teachers were treated. "I saw the injustice of paying stupid men double and treble women's wages for teaching merely because they were men," she later told a journalist, with characteristic snap. Though it was the first infuriating "seed for thought" that compelled her to fight for women's rights, it certainly wasn't the last.

Born in 1820, Susan grew up in a Quaker family that was opposed to slavery and drinking. Unlike many people at the time, her family believed that girls should be as fully educated as boys. Following in her father's footsteps, Susan campaigned against slavery and drinking. There were no laws barring drunken husbands from abusing their wives, so she saw drinking alcohol as another means of oppressing women. Susan had a gift for fiery oratory—people eventually paid to hear her speeches. She used this gift to get others excited about the issues she cared about. Susan formed a temperance (anti-alcohol) organization with her good friend and fellow rabble-rouser, Elizabeth Cady Stanton. Their hope was to get the New York State Legislature to pass a law regulating and limiting the sale of liquor. They gathered almost 30,000 signatures on a petition, but when they presented it to state legislators, the legislators ignored the petition because most of the signees were women and children.

Elizabeth spoke about women's rights at the temperance meetings. She even spoke about women being able to divorce their husbands if they drank too much. Advocating for divorce laws was shocking to many members of the temperance union. Many of them, men and women, did not get behind Elizabeth and Susan's fight for women's rights. Elizabeth was voted out as the group's president. Irate, Susan stepped down as the secretary. But Elizabeth urged her not to lose steam over these slights: "Now, Susan," she reminded her friend, "we have other and bigger fish to fry."

Susan turned to fighting even more vigorously for women's rights, including the rights of married women to own property and conduct business independently from their husbands. Yet more and more, she realized that helping women earn voting rights—the big fish of female empowerment—was the only way to guarantee that women would have a say in shaping laws that impacted their safety and status in society.

Her campaign for women's suffrage also suffered setbacks. During the Civil War, Susan helped some of her abolitionist (antislavery) allies in Congress by building support for the Thirteenth Amendment to the Constitution. The amendment, abolishing slavery, was signed into law in 1865. Susan hoped that her friends in Congress would reward her work to end slavery by moving on quickly to give women the vote. However, when the Fourteenth Amendment was ratified in 1868, it notably granted all *male* citizens over 21 the right to vote. Susan was livid!

But even when her cause hit big stumbling blocks and things weren't changing fast enough for others to recognize, Susan still saw promising advances in the long fight for equal voting rights. Once a reporter asked her how she weathered defeats, and she shot back,

"Defeats? There have been none in my life and work. . . . We are always progressing." In 1868, she and Elizabeth cofounded a feminist newspaper, *The Revolution*. It ran essays championing everything from equal pay to women's right to wear pants. In 1872, Susan cast a presidential ballot illegally and was arrested for her protest vote—a move that earned her even more fans. And she spent the next three decades speaking, organizing, and traveling across the United States and Europe, pushing for women's voting rights. Her unwavering commitment inspired tens of thousands of women to join the cause and helped several states pass their own voting rights laws.

Susan died in 1906. A month earlier, she had told a group of suffragists who'd gathered to celebrate her 86th birthday, "Failure is impossible." It was her last public statement, a famous line now printed on coffee cups and necklaces. And she did not fail. In 1920, Congress finally ratified the Nineteenth Amendment, also known as the Susan B. Anthony Amendment, granting all American women the right to vote.

> **"ORGANIZE, AGITATE, EDUCATE, MUST BE OUR WAR CRY."**

LEARN MORE!

The following books, YouTube videos, and websites may be useful to you if you want to learn more about inspiring women activists—or if you want to get started fighting for a cause of your own!

BOOKS

Being Jazz: My Life as a (Transgender) Teen by Jazz Jennings (Ember, 2016).

Girls Resist! A Guide to Activism, Leadership, and Starting a Revolution by KaeLyn Rich, illustrated by Giulia Sagramola (Quirk Books, 2018).

Heroes of the Environment by Harriet Rohmer, illustrated by Julie McLaughlin (Chronicle, 2009).

I Am Malala (Young Readers Edition) by Malala Yousafzai, with Patricia McCormick (Little, Brown Books for Young Readers, 2016).

Let It Shine by Andrea Davis Pinkney, illustrated by Stephen Alcorn (HMH Books for Young Readers, 2013).

Marley Dias Gets It Done: And So Can You! by Marley Dias, with Siobhan McGowan (Scholastic Press, 2018).

My Life with the Chimpanzees by Jane Goodall (Aladdin, 1996).

Rosa Parks: My Story by Rosa Parks with Jim Haskins (Puffin Books, 1999).

She Did It! 21 Women Who Changed the Way We Think by Emily Arnold McCully (Disney Hyperion, 2018).

Start Now! You Can Make a Difference by Chelsea Clinton, illustrated by Siobhán Gallagher (Philomel, 2018).

What Is the Women's Rights Movement? by Deborah Hopkinson, illustrated by Laurie A. Conley (Penguin Workshop, 2018).

You Are Mighty: A Guide to Changing the World by Caroline Paul, illustrated by Lauren Tamaki (Bloomsbury Children's Books, 2018).

YOUTUBE

Ask an Autistic—series by Amythest Schaber

Ask an Undocumented Girl—series by Teen Vogue

Little by Little

WEBSITES

cpdaction.org

dosomething.org/us

generationon.org

townhallproject.com

 Generation Girl books celebrate amazing women who've been there, done that, and learned some valuable lessons along the way. Be inspired by their stories, learn from their struggles and successes, and get ready to change the world. Look for more hard-won wisdom in: